God's Abundant Table

God's Abundant Table

Cynthia M. Campbell

Witherspoon
PRESS

Louisville, Kentucky

Published by Witherspoon Press, a ministry of the General Assembly Council, Presbyterian Church (U.S.A.), 100 Witherspoon St., Louisville, Kentucky.

PRINTED IN THE UNITED STATES OF AMERICA

gamc.pcusa.org/ministries/curriculum/witherspoon-press/

"For all that has been 'Thanks!' For all that will be 'Yes!'"

Dag Hamerskjold

Introduction

According to John Calvin, the true church was wherever the Word was rightly preached and the sacraments rightly administered. Put another way, church happens when believers gather to tell the story and break the bread. Calvin himself thought that the Lord's Supper should be observed every Sunday as a regular part of worship. We should hear the gospel proclaimed and then participate in the good news acted out. For a variety of reasons, weekly communion never became the norm among Presbyterian and Reformed Christians. Many of us grew up in congregations that celebrated the Lord's Supper quarterly. Only within the last thirty years has the church begun to recognize the importance of regular communion and provided a wealth of resources for congregations to recover this basic practice of worship and prayer.

This Bible Study begins from the premise that the Eucharist (the "thanksgiving meal" of the church) is far more than a reenactment of the meal in the Upper Room. Rightly understood, the Lord's Supper is connected to Jesus' entire ministry, to the entire story of God's relationship with God's people, to our everyday meals, and to the ministry to which each of us is called as Christ's followers. Over the course of these reflections, you will be invited to discover the many connections in the Bible between what we do in the Lord's Supper, what it means to be in relationship with God, and how God would have us live every day.

Each chapter includes seven selections that are designed to be read daily. A study guide follows the sixth chapter, adding further reflection on the theme, as well as suggestions for conversation and worship that might be used with a group that has covenanted to follow the study. This study is appropriate for the season of Lent but may also be used at other times for those desiring to reflect more deeply on God's presence with us whenever bread is broken.

Chapter 1

Bread Everywhere

Bless the LORD

I will bless the LORD at all times;
*   his praise shall continually be in my mouth. . . .*
I sought the LORD, and he answered me,
*   and delivered me from all my fears. . . .*
O taste and see that the LORD is good;
*   happy are those who take refuge in him.*
                                    —Psalm 34:1, 4, 8

Once you start to look for it, you find bread all over the Bible. Famine, the failure of wheat and other grain crops due to drought, is a frequent part of the drama of the Bible. It is what leads the Israelites to Egypt where they will eventually be enslaved. Liberated from slavery, Israel faces starvation in the desert wilderness until God provides "bread from heaven," the miraculous manna that appears daily and lasts only a day. When he is fleeing for his life, the prophet Elijah falls exhausted into a deep sleep. When he awakes, God commands him to get up and eat bread for the journey that has appeared miraculously. The prophet Isaiah invites God's people to feast on God's goodness freely given and asks: "Why do you spend your money for that which is not bread, and your labor for that which does not satisfy?"

Bread—breaking it, sharing it—is at the center of Jesus' story as well. Six times in the four Gospels, we read the story of the multiplication of loaves and fishes. In John's Gospel, some of the meanings that hover around this miracle are made explicit. Jesus not only provides bread for the crowd—Jesus himself is the "bread that has come down from heaven" or "the bread of life."

Near what seems to be the end of the story, Jesus and his friends share the unleavened bread of Passover. The old symbol of the bread of freedom is transformed: "this is my body given for you," he says. And when the story of Jesus begins anew in the resurrection, two friends recognize him "in the breaking of bread."

Once you start looking for it, bread is everywhere in the Bible . . . everywhere in the story of God with God's people. The most simple and basic of foods—something men and women had been making for perhaps ten thousand years before Jesus lived—this everyday stuff turns out to be the place where God and humanity meet on a regular basis. There is only one burning bush, but bread is everywhere!

What is your favorite Bible story involving bread?

Manna from Heaven

The whole congregation of the Israelites set out from Elim; and Israel came to the wilderness of Sin, which is between Elim and Sinai, on the fifteenth day of the second month after they had departed from the land of Egypt. The whole congregation of the Israelites complained against Moses and Aaron in the wilderness. The Israelites said to them, "If only we had died by the hand of the LORD in the land of Egypt, when we sat by the fleshpots and ate our fill of bread; for you have brought us out into this wilderness to kill this whole assembly with hunger."

Then the LORD said to Moses, "I am going to rain bread from heaven for you, and each day the people shall go out and gather enough for that day. In that way I will test them, whether they will follow my instruction or not. On the sixth day, when they prepare what they bring in, it will be twice as much as they gather on other days."

In the evening quails came up and covered the camp; and in the morning there was a layer of dew around the camp. When the layer of dew lifted, there on the surface of the wilderness was a fine flaky substance, as fine as frost·on the ground.

When the Israelites saw it, they said to one another, "What is it?" For they did not know what it was.

Moses said to them, "It is the bread that the LORD has given you to eat. This is what the LORD has commanded: 'Gather as much of it as each of you needs, an omer to a person according to the number of persons, all providing for those in their own tents.'"

The Israelites did so, some gathering more, some less. But when they measured it with an omer, those who gathered much had nothing over, and those who gathered little had no shortage; they gathered as much as each of them needed.

And Moses said to them, "Let no one leave any of it over until morning."

But they did not listen to Moses; some left part of it until morning, and it bred worms and became foul. And Moses was angry with them. Morning by morning they gathered it, as much as each needed; but when the sun grew hot, it melted. . . .

The house of Israel called it manna; it was like coriander seed, white, and the taste of it was like wafers made with honey.

—Exodus 16:1–5, 13–21, 31

"Don't whine," frustrated parents say to unhappy children. "Whining won't (fill in the blank): make it cooler, get us there any faster, make the line shorter." Whining is understandable in children who don't yet understand the limits within which life takes place. Learning not to whine is generally seen as a mark of maturity in adults.

Liberated from slavery in Egypt, the people of Israel find themselves in a remote and empty wilderness. Amazing as it seems, they want to go back to slavery: at least there we "ate our fill of bread!" It is possible to imagine a number of responses that God might have had to such ungrateful whining. What God does is provide what they *want* because it is what they *need*.

The English word "manna" is an almost literal adaptation of the question the people ask when they first see the white, flaky stuff appear at dawn: *"man hu?"* "What is it?" It is *manna*—it is what it is. So emblematic has this story been in Jewish and Christian imagination that we use the phrase "manna from heaven" to mean any unexpected pleasure or gain.

Manna is what God gives hungry, frightened people at the beginning of the long journey of becoming God's people. As such, this amazing gift becomes emblematic of how God relates to us: "thou preparest a table before me in the presence of mine enemies"; "you open your hand and satisfy the desire of every living thing," the psalmists sing. When Jesus teaches his followers to pray, he instructs us to ask *each day* for the bread that (like manna) is what we need for that day. And when he speaks of prayer he says, "Is there anyone among you who, if your child asks for a fish, will give a snake instead of a fish? . . . If you then, who are evil, know how to give good gifts to your children, how much more will the heavenly Father give the Holy Spirit to those who ask him!" (Luke 11:11, 13).

What has the Lord provided for you when you most needed it?

Come to the Feast

On this mountain the Lord of hosts will make for all peoples
a feast of rich food, a feast of well-aged wines,
of rich food filled with marrow, of well-aged wines strained clear.
And he will destroy on this mountain
the shroud that is cast over all peoples,
the sheet that is spread over all nations;
he will swallow up death forever.
Then the Lord God will wipe away the tears from all faces,
and the disgrace of his people he will take away from all the earth,
for the Lord has spoken.
It will be said on that day,
Lo, this is our God; we have waited for him, so that he might
save us.
This is the Lord for whom we have waited;
let us be glad and rejoice in his salvation.
For the hand of the Lord will rest on this mountain.
—Isaiah 25:6–10a

What will it be like when all that God hopes for and intends is realized? What will it be like when the reign of God—God's kingdom—comes? Isaiah says it will be like an incredible feast, a banquet to which *all peoples* will be invited. And diets of all kinds are suspended indefinitely because the menu includes rich food and only the very finest wines!

For some of us, a banquet may conjure up formal, uncomfortable clothes, assigned seats, and long speeches. We may have images of an overabundance of foods we should not be eating in the first place. The banquet or feast image would have been heard differently for people of Isaiah's or Jesus' time when most people had barely enough food to survive and famine was a regular part of life. For them, a banquet or wedding feast would have meant something totally out of the ordinary—more than enough to eat of food that delighted the senses as well as nourished the body.

This is the kind of feast the LORD's Supper is supposed to be: "This is the joyful feast of the people of God! They will come from east and west, and from north and south, and sit at table in the kingdom of God." When we use these words to invite one another to the LORD's Table, we remind ourselves that this meal not only looks back to the Upper Room; it looks forward to the fulfillment of God's purpose of us and for all creation.

It also suggests that the mood of the Table should be one of celebration more than sadness. Of course, we come to the Table meditating on the amazing fact that, "while we were yet sinners, Christ died for us." But the point of Christ's sacrificial love was not for us to feel sadness or remorse but for us to have abundant life. Where else is abundance more vividly symbolized than in a feast?

Our celebration of the LORD's Supper looks forward to God's future: "Then, at last, all peoples will be free, all divisions healed, and with your whole creation, we will sing your praise . . ." And that will be a great feast indeed!

What does it mean to you to envision the reign of God as a banquet?

Wine to Gladden the Heart

On the third day there was a wedding in Cana of Galilee, and the mother of Jesus was there. Jesus and his disciples had also been invited to the wedding.

When the wine gave out, the mother of Jesus said to him, "They have no wine."

And Jesus said to her, "Woman, what concern is that to you and to me? My hour has not yet come."

His mother said to the servants, "Do whatever he tells you."

Now standing there were six stone water jars for the Jewish rites of purification, each holding twenty or thirty gallons.

Jesus said to them, "Fill the jars with water."

And they filled them up to the brim.

He said to them, "Now draw some out, and take it to the chief steward."

So they took it. When the steward tasted the water that had become wine, and did not know where it came from (though the servants who had drawn the water knew), the steward called the bridegroom and said to him, "Everyone serves the good wine first, and then the inferior wine after the guests have become drunk. But you have kept the good wine until now."

Jesus did this, the first of his signs, in Cana of Galilee, and revealed his glory; and his disciples believed in him.

—John 2:1–11

The transformation of water into wine is "the first of his signs, in Cana of Galilee, and revealed his glory," but what is it about Jesus that this sign is supposed to reveal? Surely, it must be something more than the mere act of changing one substance into another. If that's all it is, this is a magic trick with no more meaning than the proverbial rabbit being made to appear from a hat. John has already told us that Jesus is the One who was in the beginning with God and the "true light which enlightens everyone." How does this story make clear the nature of God's purposes?

First, this is a wedding feast. In Jesus' day, this meant an entire village (maybe more) was invited and the feast went on for several days. Then as now, this was a time for great joy and hope for the future. A new family is created, and existing families are being knit together into closer community. In addition to eating and drinking, there is music and dance, laughter and storytelling. A wedding feast is meant to be enjoyed!

Second, Jesus' action produces an embarrassment of riches. Not only are the stone jars (so carefully described) huge, the quality of the wine is judged by the expert to be exceptionally good. Wine was at the time a staple food and local product. The Bible condemns drunkenness, but it also reminds us that wine makes the heart glad. According to this story, many people are going to be glad for a long time!

If such an exuberant celebration is a sign of the in-breaking of God's reign, how do our celebrations give us a glimpse of God's presence in our lives? My husband and I gave a dinner party once where we and our guests spent over four hours at the table. They savored a wonderful meal including several bottles of wine and three pies, but what we really consumed was conversation and laughter. "The food was great," one woman said to me, "but being together like this . . . that's a miracle!"

Think about the best party you ever went to. How might this be like God's presence in your life?

The Company He Keeps

After this he went out and saw a tax collector named Levi, sitting at the tax booth; and he said to him, "Follow me." And he got up, left everything, and followed him.

Then Levi gave a great banquet for him in his house; and there was a large crowd of tax collectors and others sitting at the table with them. The Pharisees and their scribes were complaining to his disciples, saying, "Why do you eat and drink with tax collectors and sinners?"

Jesus answered, "Those who are well have no need of a physician, but those who are sick; I have come to call not the righteous but sinners to repentance."

—Luke 5:27–32

Jesus was evidently an unusual religious leader. The picture we get from the Gospels is of a man who "was always a guest." Time and again, we see Jesus being entertained by people he meets along the way. Sometimes his hosts are close friends (Mary and Martha and Lazarus). Sometimes he is the guest of a critic and you sense that the meal is roast preacher. Sometimes (as here) he is the object of the host's gratitude for a changed life.

Unlike other religious leaders of his day (and unlike many who have followed him), Jesus did not advocate specific devotional practices. Because he went to the synagogues regularly, we can assume that he and his disciples for the most part followed typical Jewish observances: prayer, fasting occasionally, giving alms, washing (ritual purification, especially hands before meals). But on more than one occasion, he and his followers are criticized for lax attention to one or more of the above: you don't fast, your disciples don't wash their hands regularly enough, you eat and drink too much (a "glutton and drunkard" are the specific charges).

Above all, Jesus and his friends received hospitality from the wrong sort of people. Here, Jesus is the guest of the man who symbolizes the Roman occupation because he collects their taxes. He is a turncoat who works for the oppressor and profits from the deal! Surely a good man, a godly man would stay far away from him and his friends.

Jesus appears to have been indiscriminate about the company he keeps—he will go wherever he is asked, talk with anyone who wants to talk to him, touch and be touched by women and men who are isolated because of illness. And he appears never to have turned down an invitation to a good party because the joy of food and fellowship is a sign of the kingdom, a glimpse into God's world that one day will be ours.

Has an invitation ever changed your life? How?

Celebrate!

"Then the son said to him, 'Father, I have sinned against heaven and before you; I am no longer worthy to be called your son.'

But the father said to his slaves, 'Quickly, bring out a robe—the best one—and put it on him; put a ring on his finger and sandals on his feet. And get the fatted calf and kill it, and let us eat and celebrate; for this son of mine was dead and is alive again; he was lost and is found!' And they began to celebrate.

"Now his elder son was in the field; and when he came and approached the house, he heard music and dancing. He called one of the slaves and asked what was going on. He replied, 'Your brother has come, and your father has killed the fatted calf, because he has got him back safe and sound.' Then he became angry and refused to go in. His father came out and began to plead with him."

—Luke 15:21–28

What happens when you mess up and know it? Do you try to hide the evidence? Invent elaborate excuses? Deny, dissemble, and hope you and everyone else will forget? Or perhaps you own up to what you did wrong and step up to take the consequences.

Jesus' very familiar story, generally known as the Parable of the Prodigal Son (and his brother), might just as well be called "the parable of unexpected consequences." The story opens as the younger son demands his inheritance, essentially declaring his father dead in advance of the fact. After wasting all his money, he decides to own up to his colossal disrespect and misjudgment, and come crawling home ready to be put to work and earn his keep.

Logic would have the father slam the door in his face or, at best, give him the most menial, low-paying job while the son earns his way back into the family. Killing the fatted calf is the last thing either of the sons expects. It humbles the younger and enrages the older.

The father, rather than the prodigal, is really the focus of this story. He has waited and watched every day for his younger son to return; the porch light, if you will, is always on. There are no conditions on the welcome. Embrace cuts off apology. A feast is declared for all! And with the one who cannot rejoice, the father pleads for him to open his heart.

A few years ago, the Roman Catholic Church developed an ad campaign with the tag line: "We are family. Welcome home." The message was that no matter why you left the church or how long you've been gone, you can always come home. Churches have defined membership in a variety of ways over the centuries, and it is important to recognize that being a Christian, following the path of Jesus, requires a way of life shaped by his example. But Christian life is first of all a relationship, and for each of us it begins and continues in the same way: with the unconditional embrace of a loving God. Welcome home.

Perhaps you or someone you know has been alienated from the church. What would it take to make you or someone else feel welcome again?

And Their Eyes Were Opened

Now on that same day two of them were going to a village called Emmaus, about seven miles from Jerusalem, and talking with each other about all these things that had happened. While they were talking and discussing, Jesus himself came near and went with them, but their eyes were kept from recognizing him.

And he said to them, "What are you discussing with each other while you walk along?"

They stood still, looking sad. Then one of them, whose name was Cleopas, answered him, "Are you the only stranger in Jerusalem who does not know the things that have taken place there in these days?"

He asked them, "What things?"

They replied, "The things about Jesus of Nazareth, who was a prophet mighty in deed and word before God and all the people, and how our chief priests and leaders handed him over to be condemned to death and crucified him. But we had hoped that he was the one to redeem Israel. Yes, and besides all this, it is now the third day since these things took place. Moreover, some women of our group astounded us. They were at the tomb early this morning, and when they did not find his body there, they came back and told us that they had indeed seen a vision of angels who said that he was alive. Some of those who were with us went to the tomb and found it just as the women had said; but they did not see him."

Then he said to them, "Oh, how foolish you are, and how slow of heart to believe all that the prophets have declared! Was it not necessary that the Messiah should suffer these things and then enter into his glory?" Then beginning with Moses and all the prophets, he interpreted to them the things about himself in all the scriptures.

As they came near the village to which they were going, he walked ahead as if he were going on. But they urged him strongly, saying, "Stay with us, because it is almost evening and the day is now nearly over." So he went in to stay with them.

When he was at the table with them, he took bread, blessed and broke it, and gave it to them. Then their eyes were opened, and they recognized him; and he vanished from their sight. They said to each other, "Were not our hearts burning within us while he was talking to us on the road, while he was opening the scriptures to us?"

That same hour they got up and returned to Jerusalem; and they found the eleven and their companions gathered together. They were saying, "The LORD has risen indeed, and he has appeared to Simon!"

Then they told what had happened on the road, and how he had been made known to them in the breaking of the bread.

—Luke 24:13–35

It is a simple, everyday action—taking a small, flat loaf of bread (probably much like pita bread), saying a blessing, breaking it into pieces, and giving one to each person at the table. The father or oldest man at the meal generally did this in Jewish life. They had seen Jesus do it scores of times whenever they had eaten together. The more their lives as teacher and disciples were bound together, the more this everyday act took on deeper meaning. Eating together came to symbolize the life they were sharing together and the vision of the new life he was teaching them about.

After his death, the devastation was impossible even to verbalize. The disciples began to scatter. Two of them, walking away from Jerusalem, are overtaken by a stranger. In response to their distress, he begins to reinterpret the Scriptures they think they know, but even when he speaks, they do not recognize him. Not until he takes bread, and after giving thanks, breaks it and gives it to them.

Centuries later, far removed from the places where Jesus and his followers lived, we are invited to recognize him in just the same way—when bread is broken and shared. The LORD's Supper or Eucharist is the church's ritual act that provides the occasion for us to understand who Jesus is and what it means to be invited into relationship with him. We are invited to remember far more than the meal in the Upper Room on the night of arrest and trial and torture. We are invited to remember all the meals—dinners with friends, times of laughter, conversations shared, hopes envisioned for a world where all are welcome and all are fed.

Because the breaking of bread is the central act of our faith, we are invited to see all the rest of our meals as occasions when Christ can be known. The most ordinary thing we do—prepare food and eat it—can be the opportunity to recognize and experience the life God wants for us—the joyful feast of the people of God.

Chapter 2

Hospitality

Angels Unaware

The LORD appeared to Abraham by the oaks of Mamre, as he sat at the entrance of his tent in the heat of the day. He looked up and saw three men standing near him. When he saw them, he ran from the tent entrance to meet them, and bowed down to the ground.

He said, "My lord, if I find favor with you, do not pass by your servant. Let a little water be brought, and wash your feet, and rest yourselves under the tree. Let me bring a little bread, that you may refresh yourselves, and after that you may pass on—since you have come to your servant."

So they said, "Do as you have said."

And Abraham hastened into the tent to Sarah, and said, "Make ready quickly three measures of choice flour, knead it, and make cakes." Abraham ran to the herd, and took a calf, tender and good, and gave it to the servant, who hastened to prepare it. Then he took curds and milk and the calf that he had prepared, and set it before them; and he stood by them under the tree while they ate.

They said to him, "Where is your wife Sarah?"

And he said, "There, in the tent."

Then one said, "I will surely return to you in due season, and your wife Sarah shall have a son."

And Sarah was listening at the tent entrance behind him. Now Abraham and Sarah were old, advanced in age; it had ceased to be with Sarah after the manner of women. So Sarah laughed to herself, saying, "After I have grown old, and my husband is old, shall I have pleasure?"

The LORD said to Abraham, "Why did Sarah laugh, and say, 'Shall I indeed bear a child, now that I am old?' Is anything too wonderful for the LORD? At the set time I will return to you, in due season, and Sarah shall have a son."

But Sarah denied, saying, "I did not laugh"; for she was afraid. He said, "Oh yes, you did laugh."

—Genesis 18:1–15

"Come by and see us anytime! The coffee pot is always on." So said many members of the first congregation I served in Dallas, Texas. And when I wanted to see them, I called to make an appointment. After a couple of months, I learned that my behavior was regarded as rude. They had invited me to stop by and when I called first, it appeared that I did not take them at their word. I, however, was raised in a family where no one ever "stopped by." Visits were carefully planned so that everyone would be ready.

Out of nowhere, three strangers turn up where Abraham and Sarah have made camp. The text tells us that it is the Lord, but what Abraham *sees* is three travelers in the heat of the day. Unlike our modern world where speaking to strangers is discouraged, the custom of the desert is that the traveler is to be welcomed. No one is ever turned away. As the story unfolds, the strangers deliver the message that old Abraham and Sarah will indeed have a child in fulfillment of God's promise.

Providing hospitality to strangers has been a hallmark of Christian life from the beginning. The author of the letter to the Hebrews uses the story of Abraham as ethical precedent: "Do not neglect to show hospitality to strangers, for by doing that some have entertained angels without knowing it" (13:2).

Hospitality is at the heart of Christian vocation for the women and men who have lived as Benedictine nuns and monks. One of them writes that hospitality means being open to the stranger, but this "is not equivalent to leaving your door unlocked. . . . [It] does not mean you ignore obvious threats to personal safety. Hospitality means bringing strangers into your heart, which may or may not result in inviting strangers to the table. Do not harden your heart against suffering. Widen your boundaries to include those who are not like you."[1]

**What does hospitality mean to you? How was
it practiced in the home you grew up in?**

Mary and Martha

Now as they went on their way, he entered a certain village, where a woman named Martha welcomed him into her home. She had a sister named Mary, who sat at the Lord's feet and listened to what he was saying.

God's Abundant Table

But Martha was distracted by her many tasks; so she came to him and asked, "Lord, do you not care that my sister has left me to do all the work by myself? Tell her then to help me."

But the Lord answered her, "Martha, Martha, you are worried and distracted by many things; there is need of only one thing. Mary has chosen the better part, which will not be taken away from her."

—Luke 10:38–42

There are two aspects of hospitality—making and serving the food and being present to the guests. Unless one employs a cook or hires a caterer, someone is always in the kitchen while someone else is making conversation. Both aspects of hospitality are necessary for making people welcome. Nowadays, however, concern about the inequality of tasks has led to a more informal style of hospitality in which hosts and guests often work and talk together in the kitchen.

Jesus has come to Martha's home. Although Luke does not place this story in a particular location, it is reasonable to assume that these two sisters are the same friends of Jesus we meet in John's Gospel. In that version, they live in Bethany with their brother Lazarus, and it seems that Jesus stays in their home when visiting Jerusalem.

One of the things that is so endearing about this story is how ordinary it is. Jesus doesn't just have disciples; he has friends—friends who are close enough that he can just drop by. When he arrives, he knows he will receive both kinds of hospitality. Food *and* friendship, nourishment *and* conversation—all are essential to healthy human life.

The practice of Shabbat (Sabbath) among observant Jews captures the dual nature of hospitality perfectly. Shabbat begins at sundown on Friday. The goal is to have the meal entirely prepared and cooked in advance so that the Sabbath "rest" can be maintained. But interestingly enough, this practice allows the one who has prepared the meal to be fully present to the guests. It is a special blessing for Jews to invite friends to share this time. The meal begins with prayers, singing, ritual washing of hands, and the blessing and sharing of bread and wine. If children are present, their parents bless them. Then there is dinner. The point is to linger at the table, to enjoy food and conversation throughout the evening—to rest together and to be nourished by both food and friendship.

As you entertain others, when are you like Martha and when are you like Mary? How do these two roles feel to you?

Companions

Your steadfast love, O LORD, extends to the heavens,
*   your faithfulness to the clouds.*
Your righteousness is like the mighty mountains,
*   your judgments are like the great deep;*
*   you save humans and animals alike, O LORD.*
How precious is your steadfast love, O God!
*   All people may take refuge in the shadow of your wings.*
They feast on the abundance of your house,
*   and you give them drink from the river of your delights.*
For with you is the fountain of life;
*   in your light we see light.*

                                                —Psalm 36:5–9

We need food but also friendship to survive. Bread is food that is meant to be shared—broken into pieces and shared with people who become "companions," literally those with bread.

This came home to me vividly last year. My 99-year-old father lives in a retirement community in California. I arrived from Chicago to discover that the health department had closed the dining room because several residents had come down with the flu. The drill, as my father explained it, was that we were to decide what we wanted from the menu, call down to the desk, and it would be delivered around 6 p.m. We got what you might imagine—not-very-warm stuff in plastic containers.

One night of this was enough! Fortunately, my father is in great shape and enjoys eating out. As the days wore on, however, I began to get really eager for the dining room to reopen. It's not that the food is spectacular (although as institutional food goes, it is well prepared, nutritious, and full of variety). The issue really was the dining room. Since my mother died three years ago, my father has eaten every evening meal with three women, all widows. Nancy is a longtime member of our church. Dee moved in with her husband around the same time my parents did over twenty years ago. Margie is the "newcomer" who arrived about the time my mother died. The four of them have a regular table, and I join them whenever I visit. Somewhere on day two of this exile from the dining room, I began to realize how deeply I missed our evening meal together.

The day before I left, the dining room finally reopened. We reserved a table, and shortly after 5 p.m., we all arrived. "I feel like I've been let out of jail!" Margie exclaimed. And so did we all. In those days everyone became vividly aware that the dining room isn't just about food, necessary as that is. It's about *companionship*—the breaking and sharing of bread.

What is the difference between eating and feasting?

Crumbs from the Table

From there he set out and went away to the region of Tyre. He entered a house and did not want anyone to know he was there. Yet he could not escape notice, but a woman whose little daughter had an unclean spirit immediately heard about him, and she came and bowed down at his feet. Now the woman was a Gentile, of Syrophoenician origin. She begged him to cast the demon out of her daughter.

He said to her, "Let the children be fed first, for it is not fair to take the children's food and throw it to the dogs."

But she answered him, "Sir, even the dogs under the table eat the children's crumbs."

Then he said to her, "For saying that, you may go—the demon has left your daughter."

So she went home, found the child lying on the bed, and the demon gone.

—Mark 7:24–30

Most societies put boundaries on relationships, boundaries that define with whom it is appropriate to associate or do business or marry. And while we live in a time when many of these boundaries are disappearing, others have taken on new importance. Marrying across racial or cultural lines is now common, but we have heightened concern about professional boundaries and conflicts of interest in business dealings.

Jesus lived in a time and culture where boundaries were crucial to identity. Three times in this passage, Mark calls attention to the fact that Jesus and his disciples have crossed some of these boundaries: they have journeyed outside the territory of Israel to the region (north and near the Mediterranean) of Tyre. There they meet a woman of that region, who is doubly identified as "other"—a Gentile of Syrophoenician origin.

The interchange between the woman and Jesus is perhaps the least flattering story in all the Gospels. "It is not fair to take the children's food and throw it to the dogs," he says in response to her plea that he heal her daughter. Jesus, who "loves all the little children of the world," has just called this woman's child a dog! How is that even possible? And if it happened this way, why on earth would the tradition remember this incident and retell it?

Many commentators seek to get Jesus off the hook by explaining that he is "just testing her" to see if she "has faith" in him (as Matthew suggests in his version). But another reading suggests that this woman's response in fact catches Jesus up short and confronts him with the limits of his own imagination about the boundaries of God's hospitality. "Even dogs get crumbs," she replies, and everyone knows she is right!

Where do we place our boundaries? We say that all who confess Christ are welcome at the Lord's Table, but what about in membership in our congregations? Who is welcome to become an officer? Who is welcome in American society? Does this story have anything to do with immigration policy?

Unexpected Invitation

He said also to the one who had invited him, "When you give a luncheon or a dinner, do not invite your friends or your brothers or your relatives or rich neighbors, in case they may invite you in return, and you would be repaid. But when you give a banquet, invite the poor, the crippled, the lame, and the blind. And you will be blessed, because they cannot repay you, for you will be repaid at the resurrection of the righteous."

—Luke 14:12–14

Kingdom hospitality has a completely different set of rules! In the world we live in, invitations to dinner are based on family and friendship, courtship or business. And reciprocity is usually involved somehow—it's our turn to host Thanksgiving or we hope that one date will lead to another or we are thanking clients for business. There is nothing wrong with this kind of hospitality. Such occasions often bring great joy and good fellowship.

But kingdom hospitality works on another model: "invite the poor, the crippled, the lame, and the blind," Jesus says to the leader of the Pharisees who has invited him to dinner. To which the Pharisee might reasonably respond, "Haven't I done that already? How are you, who have no home of your own, going to repay me?"

Jesus' point is that the welcome that God extends has a special audience. It is not only for those "insiders" who already know and follow the path God has set out. The kingdom banquet isn't just for those who expect to attend; it is for those for whom God has particular care. Especially in Luke's Gospel, we have known from the beginning that the poor and vulnerable have a special place. In Mary's song, we hear praise for God who has "filled the hungry with good things and sent the rich away empty." Jesus inaugurates his ministry with Isaiah's proclamation of good news to the poor, a theme Jesus repeats when John's disciples come and ask him whether he is "the one who is to come" (see 7:22).

God's priorities are to become our own, obviously. "Be merciful (or compassionate), just as your Father is merciful," Jesus says (6:36). Learning how to practice kingdom hospitality takes a lifetime; it is a spiritual discipline with real-world consequences.

What happens when the church's ministry is shaped by kingdom hospitality? How would mission take on new forms? Where are the poor, the vulnerable, the isolated, the overlooked in your community? And what is your role in extending God's compassion to them?

When Did We See You?

"When the Son of Man comes in his glory, and all the angels with him, then he will sit on the throne of his glory. All the nations will be gathered before him, and he will separate people one from another as a shepherd separates the sheep from the goats, and he will put the sheep at his right hand and the goats at the left.

Then the king will say to those at his right hand, 'Come, you that are blessed by my Father, inherit the kingdom prepared for you from the foundation of the world; for I was hungry and you gave me food, I was thirsty and you gave me something to drink, I was a stranger and you welcomed me, I was naked and you gave me clothing, I was sick and you took care of me, I was in prison and you visited me.'

Then the righteous will answer him, 'Lord, when was it that we saw you hungry and gave you food, or thirsty and gave you something to drink? And when was it that we saw you a stranger and welcomed you, or naked and gave you clothing? And when was it that we saw you sick or in prison and visited you?'

And the king will answer them, 'Truly I tell you, just as you did it to one of the least of these who are members of my family, you did it to me.'

Then he will say to those at his left hand, 'You that are accursed, depart from me into the eternal fire prepared for the devil and his angels; for I was hungry and you gave me no food, I was thirsty and you gave me nothing to drink, I was a stranger and you did not welcome me, naked and you did not give me clothing, sick and in prison and you did not visit me.'

Then they also will answer, 'Lord, when was it that we saw you hungry or thirsty or a stranger or naked or sick or in prison, and did not take care of you?'

Then he will answer them, 'Truly I tell you, just as you did not do it to one of the least of these, you did not do it to me.'

And these will go away into eternal punishment, but the righteous into eternal life."

—Matthew 25:31–46

Hospitality as a Christian practice is more than entertaining. It is more than making people feel welcome. It goes beyond the serving and sharing of food. Hospitality as a Christian practice includes all the ways we reach out to those who are most vulnerable in our society. But as this parable suggests, the crucial first step is *seeing*. "When did we *see* you hungry or thirsty, a stranger or naked or sick or in prison?" We often read this sentence with the emphasis on the word "you," suggesting that the problem is that those who did not respond to those in need failed to recognize them as *Jesus*. It is just as likely that they simply didn't *see* them at all.

Poor people are easy to spot in large, urban areas. Homeless people, often begging for spare change, gather on street corners, outside restaurants, near tourist attractions. People make different moral calculations about how to respond. My husband (who always has a huge amount of spare change in his pockets) usually responds, often to people he recognizes as "regulars" in particular places. In other areas, suburbs or smaller communities, poverty and other kinds of need may not be as visible, but it is there nonetheless.

The Fourth Presbyterian Church of Chicago is located on Michigan Avenue in the midst of the city's highest-end shopping district, but the poor and vulnerable are nearby. Elam Davies, pastor from the late 1960s to the early 1980s, preached regularly about the need of that church to reach out to "the least, the last, the lost, and the left-behind." These vivid words sparked the congregation's imagination. Today a tutoring program works with more than 500 children a week from a poor neighborhood nearby. Hundreds of guests come each week to the Elam Davies Social Service Center to receive food, toiletries, clothing, a safe place to rest, counseling, and assistance in making the transition from the streets to stable housing.

Like all successful ministries of this kind, those who are serving see the others as guests—people with names and stories and hopes as well as needs.

Where are "the least, the last, the lost, and the left-behind" where you live? What might you and your congregation do for and with them?

Food and Justice

Now in the following instructions I do not commend you, because when you come together it is not for the better but for the worse. For, to begin with, when you come together as a church, I hear that there are divisions among you; and to some extent I believe it. Indeed, there have to be factions among you, for only so will it become clear who among you are genuine. When you come together, it is not really to eat the Lord's supper. For when the time comes to eat, each of you goes ahead with your own supper, and one goes hungry and another becomes drunk. What! Do you not have homes to eat and drink in? Or do you show contempt for the church of God and humiliate those who have nothing? What should I say to you? Should I commend you? In this matter I do not commend you!

Whoever, therefore, eats the bread or drinks the cup of the Lord in an unworthy manner will be answerable for the body and blood of the Lord. Examine yourselves, and only then eat of the bread and drink of the cup. For all who eat and drink without discerning the body, eat and drink judgment against themselves. For this reason many of you are weak and ill, and some have died. But if we judged ourselves, we would not be judged. But when we are judged by the Lord, we are disciplined so that we may not be condemned along with the world.

So then, my brothers and sisters, when you come together to eat, wait for one another. If you are hungry, eat at home, so that when you come together, it will not be for your condemnation. About the other things I will give instructions when I come.

—1 Corinthians 11:17–22, 27–34

The hospitality God extends to us and expects from us is inextricably bound to justice, as this letter from Paul to the church in Corinth makes clear. Reading the passage carefully, we can imagine that this community of believers gathers for the Lord's Supper and for a meal. It appears that some arrive early and eat most of the food so that those who arrive later are left with little or nothing. Many scholars suggest that the late arrivals are probably servants or even slaves who have less control over their time.

What is interesting is that Paul sees this behavior not only as bad manners but also as a violation of the integrity of the Lord's Supper. When some have enough and others are hungry, those who have no food are humiliated and the integrity of the church is in question. Paul concludes with a stern warning that "all who eat and drink without *discerning the body,* eat and drink judgment against themselves." For centuries, these words have been used in theological debates about how the bread used in communion becomes (or doesn't) the "body of Christ." Usually, however, when Paul uses the phrase "the body of Christ," he is talking about the church. Thus, the point is perhaps more accurately: whoever shares in the Lord's Supper and does not recognize the needs and dignity of the others at the table stands liable to God's judgment.

Food and justice are inevitably linked together. This was dramatically demonstrated during the civil rights movement. One of the first forms of protest was the attempt to integrate lunch counters in drugstores across the South. Segregation defined who could be served where and who could eat with whom. Black and white college students broke the law by going to eat together. They made America see blatant injustice by appealing to a deep sense of the connection between food and hospitality and justice for all.

Many have said that every human being has a basic right to have enough to eat. Do you agree or disagree? If you agree, how would a society make sure everyone does have enough to eat?

Chapter 3

Just Eating

Gleaning

When you reap your harvest in your field and forget a sheaf in the field, you shall not go back to get it; it shall be left for the alien, the orphan, and the widow, so that the LORD your God may bless you in all your undertakings. When you beat your olive trees, do not strip what is left; it shall be for the alien, the orphan, and the widow.

When you gather the grapes of your vineyard, do not glean what is left; it shall be for the alien, the orphan, and the widow. Remember that you were a slave in the land of Egypt; therefore I am commanding you to do this.

—Deuteronomy 24:19–22

Food is a necessity for everything that lives. In the human world, food is also a matter of justice. This passage from the Law of Moses (or Torah) imagines Israel as an agrarian culture where grain, olives, and grapes are the staple crops. It also imagines that, in addition to those who work the land and are able to live by virtue of what they raise and sell, others do not have ready access to food. This passage names them as "the alien, the orphan, and the widow." These persons could not own land or did not belong to an extended family within which food would be provided. Thus, Torah provides a means by which widows, orphans, and resident aliens can get access to food. They are permitted to come in after the harvest and take what remains. In fact, the owner/harvester is commanded not to harvest the entire crop precisely so that there is something left. One might call this a prototype of food stamps.

The reason for the law is straightforward but repeated in a number of other cases. Israel is to provide for these people on the margins because of their own experience: Israel was enslaved, aliens living in Egypt. God's redemptive action on their behalf sets up an economy of obligation: "Do for others what God has done for you."

The assumption behind this law is not charity but justice. Charity is what we give freely to or for the benefit of others. Justice is treating others fairly. This law assumes that making it possible for everyone to have enough food to eat is what is right. It is what the virtuous society should do—it should, as a matter of law, make sure that everyone has the basic necessities. Amazingly enough, this is not a universally held conviction, even among those who claim that the Bible is the basis for the moral life.

What is the modern equivalent of these provisions from Deuteronomy? Why is there resistance to giving everyone equal access to enough food to eat?

Open to Impossibilities

Then the word of the LORD came to him, saying, "Go now to Zarephath, which belongs to Sidon, and live there; for I have commanded a widow there to feed you."

So he set out and went to Zarephath. When he came to the gate of the town, a widow was there gathering sticks; he called to her and said, "Bring me a little water in a vessel, so that I may drink." As she was going to bring it, he called to her and said, "Bring me a morsel of bread in your hand."

But she said, "As the LORD your God lives, I have nothing baked, only a handful of meal in a jar, and a little oil in a jug; I am now gathering a couple of sticks, so that I may go home and prepare it for myself and my son, that we may eat it, and die."

Elijah said to her, "Do not be afraid; go and do as you have said; but first make me a little cake of it and bring it to me, and afterwards make something for yourself and your son. For thus says the LORD the God of Israel: The jar of meal will not be emptied and the jug of oil will not fail until the day that the LORD sends rain on the earth."

She went and did as Elijah said, so that she as well as he and her household ate for many days. The jar of meal was not emptied, neither did the jug of oil fail, according to the word of the LORD that he spoke by Elijah.

—1 Kings 17:8–16

God does not want people to starve. But what happens when food supplies give out? When drought devastates an already poor country? When food aid becomes part of a complex tangle of international relations? When nations give up food production in favor of production of other crops for export and then are forced to buy food at prices they cannot afford?

God does not want people to starve. But in the richest nation in the world, people are hungry, and the demand for food assistance grew significantly during the recent recession. The reality of hungry people in a nation of plenty raises questions of both charity and justice.

In the reading, the prophet Elijah is at the beginning of his career of conflict with Israel's King Ahab over the king's loyalty (or lack thereof) to God. As this chapter opens, a severe drought is spreading across the land. In the first scene, Elijah goes out to the wilderness and survives by the bank of a small stream. When that dries up, God leads him to a Gentile region, to a poor widow in the village of Zarephath. This woman and her young son are almost a stereotype of extreme poverty in a land where most people are subsistence farmers. Her resources have run out; she is as exhausted as her supplies of grain and oil. The next step is to wait for starvation, to keep watch as she and her son die.

From out of nowhere, Elijah appears. He is not one of her people; he is a foreigner, a stranger. In the middle of this great drought, he asks her for water. Rather than walk away turning a deaf ear, she gets water for him. Despite her utter destitution, her first instinct is to respond to another in need.

This poor woman's hospitality sets the stage for God's miracle. Her willingness to reach out to another in need opens the way for God's provision of grain and oil that will not run out. God doesn't want people to starve; neither should we.

What should be done about starvation?

Feed Them

Now when Jesus heard this, he withdrew from there in a boat to a deserted place by himself. But when the crowds heard it, they followed him on foot from the towns. When he went ashore, he saw a great crowd; and he had compassion for them and cured their sick.

When it was evening, the disciples came to him and said, "This is a deserted place, and the hour is now late; send the crowds away so that they may go into the villages and buy food for themselves."

Jesus said to them, "They need not go away; you give them something to eat."

They replied, "We have nothing here but five loaves and two fish."

And he said, "Bring them here to me."

Then he ordered the crowds to sit down on the grass. Taking the five loaves and the two fish, he looked up to heaven, and blessed and broke the loaves, and gave them to the disciples, and the disciples gave them to the crowds. And all ate and were filled; and they took up what was left over of the broken pieces, twelve baskets full. And those who ate were about five thousand men, besides women and children.

—Matthew 14:13–21

Twice, the text emphasizes that they are in a "deserted place." Jesus has set out to find a place for reflection after learning of the death of John the Baptist. But when the crowds figure out where he is headed, they arrive ahead of him. The region may be desolate (or "lonely" as the RSV puts it), but it is filled with hungry people. First, they are hungry for Jesus and his teaching—that is what has lured the crowd out beyond the confines of village and town. But later, they are simply hungry, and the disciples want Jesus to send them away from the place of desolation back to where they can all find proper food.

Jesus, however, wants to make a point about God and food. Not only does God not want people to starve; God has regularly shown God's presence, power, and compassion by feeding God's people in the wilderness, in deserted places. Just as God fed manna to the people of Israel after their escape from Egypt; just as God provided food for Elijah (on more than one occasion) when he was at risk of losing his life; just so Jesus now feeds the crowd. What he refused to do for himself in his temptation (see Matthew 4:1–4), he now does for the crowd. It is not magic; it is a mysterious gesture pointing to God's purpose and presence.

Hundreds of thousands of Americans live in "food deserts," urban neighborhoods in which there is no ready access to fresh food (meat, fish, poultry, dairy products, fruits, and vegetables). In the food desert, what is readily available is "fast food"—packaged and processed food—and alcohol. There is an epidemic of obesity in the United States, and many of those affected are urban poor who have little or no access to healthful food.

One solution is year-round farmers' markets in poor neighborhoods. Farmers' markets have long been popular in upscale city neighborhoods where fresh produce vies with flowers and designer cheeses, but this more recent movement brings healthy food to those least likely to have access to it.

Who would Jesus feed?

Bread in the Desert

In those days when there was again a great crowd without anything to eat, he called his disciples and said to them, "I have compassion for the crowd, because they have been with me now for three days and have nothing to eat. If I send them away hungry to their homes, they will faint on the way—and some of them have come from a great distance."

His disciples replied, "How can one feed these people with bread here in the desert?"

He asked them, "How many loaves do you have?"

They said, "Seven."

Then he ordered the crowd to sit down on the ground; and he took the seven loaves, and after giving thanks he broke them and gave them to his disciples to distribute; and they distributed them to the crowd. They had also a few small fish; and after blessing them, he ordered that these too should be distributed. They ate and were filled;

and they took up the broken pieces left over, seven baskets full. Now there were about four thousand people. And he sent them away. And immediately he got into the boat with his disciples and went to the district of Dalmanutha.

—Mark 8:1–10

When Jesus is around, a little bit of food becomes enough to satisfy a huge crowd. When Jesus is around, anyone and everyone is fed. These two ideas are at the heart of the feeding stories. Mark tells them twice (Matthew follows suit; Luke and John do not). There are minor variations, but the outline is the same. The importance of these stories in the imagination of the first Christians cannot be overemphasized. Before there were depictions of Christ on the cross (later the dominant image of Jesus), there were carvings and frescos of this scene: Jesus with basket upon basket of bread and fish.

The idea that God should be equated with abundance rather than scarcity is not always at the core of our religious experience. We live in a world obsessed with scarcity and thus anxious about getting and protecting what we think rightly belongs to us. In the feeding stories, Jesus feeds the whole crowd—and then there are the leftovers. Preachers often imagine that some people had food with them but were reluctant to share until Jesus started passing out bread. However it happened, the miracle is one of divine abundance—the symbol of God's creative energy and imagination. As we read, we are invited to receive and share, to set down our anxieties about whether there will be enough and simply be nourished.

The idea of radical welcome is even more challenging to those of us who like our world sorted out into those who rightly belong and those who do not. The church has long struggled with this as well. On one level, we can imagine good reasons for naming and keeping certain boundaries on Christian community. In times when the church is under persecution, it is important to know that those who come in are genuine and not seeking to do harm. But most of the time, the barriers we have placed to and around the Table seem at odds with Jesus' own habit of welcoming all and receiving the welcome of any.

Who should come to the Lord's Table?
Who should be admitted to Christian
fellowship? Should there be any limits?

I Must Stay at Your House

He entered Jericho and was passing through it. A man was there named Zacchaeus; he was a chief tax collector and was rich. He was trying to see who Jesus was, but on account of the crowd he could not, because he was short in stature. So he ran ahead and climbed a sycamore tree to see him, because he was going to pass that way.

When Jesus came to the place, he looked up and said to him, "Zacchaeus, hurry and come down; for I must stay at your house today."

So he hurried down and was happy to welcome him. All who saw it began to grumble and said, "He has gone to be the guest of one who is a sinner."

    Zacchaeus stood there and said to the Lord, "Look, half of my possessions, Lord, I will give to the poor; and if I have defrauded anyone of anything, I will pay back four times as much."

    Then Jesus said to him, "Today salvation has come to this house, because he too is a son of Abraham. For the Son of Man came to seek out and to save the lost."

—Luke 19:1–10

This time, Jesus invites himself to dinner, and the life of the spontaneous host is transformed. Zacchaeus, whom a Sunday school song calls "a wee little man," was a villain to his neighbors—the collector of the despised tax owed to the Roman occupiers. One could become rich managing financial affairs for the oppressive empire, and Zacchaeus had done just that. Having sold out his family and neighbors, the designation "sinner" was probably a mild epithet at best.

    But he wants to see Jesus, and when Jesus sees him in the tree, he announces that he and his friends are ready to accept Zacchaeus' hospitality. Somewhere between that meeting and dessert at the end of the meal, Zacchaeus' life is transformed by eating with Jesus. In his public announcement, he promises what the rich ruler (Luke 18:18–25) was unable to do: he will sell his possessions and give the money to the poor.

In her recent book, Take This Bread: A Radical Conversion, writer Sara Miles describes the transformation of her life after the day she wandered into a small Episcopal church in San Francisco: "Eating Jesus, as I did that day to my great astonishment, led me against all my expectations to a faith I'd scorned and work I'd never imagined. . . . I took communion, I passed the bread to others, and then I kept going, compelled to find new ways to share what I'd experienced."[2]

From there, Miles went on to share what she had eaten by opening food pantries across the area, enabling poor people to get fresh fruits and vegetables. The more she became involved in feeding people, the deeper became her connection to Christian faith.

Eating with Jesus can be dangerous; it can turn your life inside out.

What is God calling you to change about your life?

Enough for All

Awe came upon everyone, because many wonders and signs were being done by the apostles. All who believed were together and had all things in common; they would sell their possessions and goods and distribute the proceeds to all, as any had need.

—Acts 2:43–45

Of all the possible ways that the first believers might have responded to the message of new life through the Risen Jesus, the one described here is curious. Why did baptism lead to communal living? The Gospels do not record any specific instructions from Jesus about what shape the life of his followers should take. Even if this picture of the earliest church is a romanticized reconstruction rather than an on-the-scene account, other evidence suggests that a "shared meal" tradition was common among believers in cities around the Mediterranean. What links these other accounts to the passage in Acts is the practice of sharing. People apparently brought whatever they had, and everyone ended up with enough to eat.

Part of the problem with the global food supply is the great inequity of distribution. Some of us have pretty much whatever we want whenever we want it; others die of malnutrition or starvation. The United States is one of the world's largest producers of food, but hunger is a major issue. According to Bread for the World, 14.6 percent of all U.S. households struggle to put food on the table; this translates to forty-nine million Americans and 16.7 million children (based on USDA statistics). The Supplemental Nutrition Assistance Program, or SNAP, is a government program aiding families with food needs. Nearly half of all American children will receive SNAP benefits at some point before they are twenty years old. Among African Americans, that figure is 90 percent. For most families, SNAP benefits are used up by the third week of the month.[3]

The United States is also one of the most religiously active or observant nations in the world, and the majority of Americans identify themselves as members of some religious community, most of them Christian. Surely, such statistics about hunger are at odds with the core teachings of all religious traditions, but they should be especially troubling for a tradition where one of the first responses to the resurrection of Jesus was to feed hungry people.

Scholars suggest that one reason the first followers of Jesus gathered in Jerusalem, pooled their resources, and shared food was that they expected Jesus would return at any moment. Could such sharing become a mark of Christian practice today?

Just Service

Now during those days, when the disciples were increasing in number, the Hellenists complained against the Hebrews because their widows were being neglected in the daily distribution of food.

And the twelve called together the whole community of the disciples and said, "It is not right that we should neglect the word of God in order to wait on tables. Therefore, friends, select from among yourselves seven men of good standing, full of the Spirit and of wisdom, whom we may appoint to this task, while we, for our part, will devote ourselves to prayer and to serving the word."

What they said pleased the whole community, and they chose Stephen, a man full of faith and the Holy Spirit, together with Philip, Prochorus, Nicanor, Timon, Parmenas, and Nicolaus, a proselyte of Antioch. They had these men stand before the apostles, who prayed and laid their hands on them.

—Acts 6:1–6

The office of deacon (literally "the server") has its origin in a crisis of the early church. The new community of believers in Jerusalem has already been described as one in which "there was not a needy person among them" (4:34). But apparently this was not entirely the case. Although all are Jewish Christians, the tension seems to be between two groups differentiated by language (Greek-speaking Hellenists and Aramaic-speaking Hebrews). The first group complains that their widows have not been receiving an equal share of the distributed food.[4]

Care for widows was an integral part of Jewish life and clearly defined as the church continued the practice. What is notable about this story is the way the leaders moved quickly to solve the crisis by proposing a solution to the whole community: select "men of good standing," and the leaders will commission them to make sure that this important need in the community's life is met.

The Book of Order defines the office of deacon as one of "sympathy, witness, and service after the example of Jesus Christ." Specifically, deacons are to "minister to those in need, to the sick, to the friendless, and to any who may be in distress both within and beyond the community of faith" (G-6.0400).

From the very beginning, Christian community has called forth leaders not only to teach the faith but to serve the real, physical needs of its own people and of the world. Deacons remind us that it is not enough simply to preach good news to the poor. The hungry need food; the naked need clothing; those who are sick or lonely or shut-up in prison or shut-in at home need visitors—people who will show up and sit down and listen and care.

Christianity is about sharing the Bread of Life—Jesus; about sharing the bread that is his body in worship; about sharing bread— real food—with hungry people.

Complete equity is almost never possible, but what are some of the barriers you see that keep some people from sharing with others?

Chapter 4

Food for the Spirit

The Bread of Life

So they said to him, "What sign are you going to give us then, so that we may see it and believe you? What work are you performing? Our ancestors ate the manna in the wilderness; as it is written, 'He gave them bread from heaven to eat.' "

Then Jesus said to them, "Very truly, I tell you, it was not Moses who gave you the bread from heaven, but it is my Father who gives you the true bread from heaven. For the bread of God is that which comes down from heaven and gives life to the world."

They said to him, "Sir, give us this bread always."

Jesus said to them, "I am the bread of life. Whoever comes to me will never be hungry, and whoever believes in me will never be thirsty.

"I am the bread of life. Your ancestors ate the manna in the wilderness, and they died. This is the bread that comes down from heaven, so that one may eat of it and not die."

—John 6:30–35, 48–50

Whereas the first three Gospels tell the story of the multiplication of the loaves and fishes, the Gospel of John makes that story the setting for a conflicted interchange in which Jesus' identity and authority are at stake. In the Synoptic Gospels, the feeding stories are like parables in action where Jesus demonstrates what the kingdom of God is like—all are welcome, all are fed, and there is more than enough to go around. Here, the feeding story is the occasion to reflect on Jesus himself through one of the several "I am" sayings so distinctive of this Gospel.

"I am the bread of life." The other "bread of life" or "bread of heaven" was the manna God provided for Israel in the wilderness after the people escaped from slavery. Now, Jesus uses that powerful story as a window onto his true identity. Just as God kept Israel alive so that they could begin to learn what it meant to live as God's holy nation, the people of the covenant, so Jesus himself is the food that will sustain believers.

Bread in the Bible is about food, about saving people from real starvation. But bread is always about more than food for the body; it is also a metaphor for what sustains and nourishes the soul. The

Christian life is nourished precisely by regular reflection on the story of Jesus in such a way that we discover our own stories through his. Ignatius Loyola urged meditating on events in Jesus' life in such a way that you put yourself into the story and imagine Jesus speaking directly to you. Imagine yourself alongside Peter and Andrew, and hear Jesus say, "Come, follow me." Or imagine yourself at the pool of Bethsaida and hear Jesus ask you, "Do you want to be made well?"

Or imagine yourself hungry and thirsty, and hear Jesus say: "Whoever comes to me will never be hungry, and whoever believes in me will never be thirsty."

For what are you most hungry?

Bread from Heaven

"I am the living bread that came down from heaven. Whoever eats of this bread will live forever; and the bread that I will give for the life of the world is my flesh."

The Jews then disputed among themselves, saying, "How can this man give us his flesh to eat?"

So Jesus said to them, "Very truly, I tell you, unless you eat the flesh of the Son of Man and drink his blood, you have no life in you. Those who eat my flesh and drink my blood have eternal life, and I will raise them up on the last day; for my flesh is true food and my blood is true drink. Those who eat my flesh and drink my blood abide in me, and I in them. Just as the living Father sent me, and I live because of the Father, so whoever eats me will live because of me. This is the bread that came down from heaven, not like that which your ancestors ate, and they died. But the one who eats this bread will live forever." He said these things while he was teaching in the synagogue at Capernaum.

When many of his disciples heard it, they said, "This teaching is difficult; who can accept it?"

—John 6:51–60

By the time the Gospel of John is written (probably in the late first century), two generations have come and gone since the events portrayed. In general, John is less interested in recording a large number of events in Jesus' life. Rather, he is concerned to interpret or reflect on the meaning of those events in extended speeches by Jesus or through editorial comments. For two generations, Christians had been baptizing and breaking bread together. We can tell from Paul's (much earlier) letters how important these practices were in shaping individual discipleship and community life. While the Synoptic Gospels tell the story of Jesus' baptism and record his words over bread and wine in the Upper Room, John does neither. Rather, he merely alludes to Jesus' baptism (1:32–34) and tells of foot-washing in the Upper Room.

It is here, in response to the feeding in the wilderness that John reflects on the meaning of the basic Christian practice of breaking bread: "Those who eat my flesh and drink my blood have eternal life, and I will raise them up on the last day; for my flesh is true food and my blood is true drink." With language like this, it's no wonder the early church had to defend itself against charges that it practiced cannibalism!

What this language lifts up is the materialism of Christian faith. In Jesus, the Word was not simply communicated or spoken (as God spoke through the prophets). In Jesus, the Word becomes flesh and blood, with all the limitations and messiness those elements imply. This is the heart of the Christian vision: though God never ceases being the Creator, the Almighty, the One who is wholly other from us and creation, nevertheless this God took on flesh and blood and lived among us as one of us.

Teachers of Christian faith have labored for two centuries to explain or express this great mystery. John invites us to experience that mystery whenever bread is broken and wine is shared. John invites us to taste and touch and savor the living God.

John goes on to recount that some were offended by Jesus' words here. Do you find them offensive, challenging, or perplexing?

Abide in Me

"I am the true vine, and my Father is the vinegrower. He removes every branch in me that bears no fruit. Every branch that bears fruit he prunes to make it bear more fruit. You have already been cleansed by the word that I have spoken to you. Abide in me as I abide in you. Just as the branch cannot bear fruit by itself unless it abides in the vine, neither can you unless you abide in me. I am the vine, you are the branches. Those who abide in me and I in them bear much fruit, because apart from me you can do nothing. Whoever does not abide in me is thrown away like a branch and withers; such branches are gathered, thrown into the fire, and burned. If you abide in me, and my words abide in you, ask for whatever you wish, and it will be done for you. My Father is glorified by this, that you bear much fruit and become my disciples.

As the Father has loved me, so I have loved you; abide in my love. If you keep my commandments, you will abide in my love, just as I have kept my Father's commandments and abide in his love. I have said these things to you so that my joy may be in you, and that your joy may be complete."

—John 15:1–11

"Abide" is one of John's favorite words. It appears in the previous passage: "Those who eat my flesh and drink my blood abide in me and I in them." The first time John uses the word sets the stage for the full meaning we find here. In 1:35–39, two of John's disciples (one of whom is identified as Andrew) come to Jesus and ask him, "Where are you staying?" Literally: "Where do you abide?" Jesus tells them to come and see; they do, and then "remain" (abide) with him. On one level, the disciples appear to be asking about where Jesus lives, but by the time we reach chapter 15, we know that there is another level of meaning here.

Where does Jesus abide? He abides deeply inside the life of God. He draws his life from God just as branches draw life through the vine and root system. To be a disciple of Jesus, then, is to draw life from him in the same way that he draws it from the One he calls "my Father." Christian life is being rooted and grounded, nourished and sustained by Christ. Over the centuries, Christians have found various practices that build up this relationship. For some, abiding in or with Jesus happens through sustained prayer or meditation; for others, it is found through the study and reflection on the Bible and the writings of great teachers of the faith; for others, abiding with Jesus is experienced when doing the work that he did in his own ministry—caring for the sick, feeding the hungry, welcoming outcasts and strangers.

Regardless of the specific practice or path we pursue, the character of the life we find is the same. Abiding in Jesus means to experience the love that he knew with God and expressed to those he encountered in life. But this abiding is not an end in itself; it has an expected outcome, namely that our lives will look like his as we learn how to love others as he loved.

When do you most feel in relationship with Jesus?

His Hour

When the hour came, he took his place at the table, and the apostles with him. He said to them, "I have eagerly desired to eat this Passover with you before I suffer; for I tell you, I will not eat it until it is fulfilled in the kingdom of God."

Then he took a cup, and after giving thanks he said, "Take this and divide it among yourselves; for I tell you that from now on I will not drink of the fruit of the vine until the kingdom of God comes."

Then he took a loaf of bread, and when he had given thanks, he broke it and gave it to them, saying, "This is my body, which is given for you. Do this in remembrance of me."

And he did the same with the cup after supper, saying, "This cup that is poured out for you is the new covenant in my blood. But see, the one who betrays me is with me, and his hand is on the table. For the Son of Man is going as it has been determined, but woe to that one by whom he is betrayed!"

Then they began to ask one another, which one of them it could be who would do this.

—Luke 22:14–23 (see also Matthew 26:20–30; Mark 14:17–26)

The setting is a meal—not an ordinary meal, but one whose food is filled with symbolic significance conveying the story of God's powerful grace in liberating Israel from slavery in Egypt. In the midst of the meal, Jesus takes bread and wine, already on the table, already shared as the Passover story was told, and gives them new meanings.

Few other Gospel passages have been given as much scrutiny or become the occasion for more (and more divisive) theological debate. All Christians use (some variation of) these words when they break the bread and pour a cup. But what do these words mean and what are we who say and hear them doing? Are we "remembering" Jesus, and if so, what are we to call to mind? Only Jesus' death? Are we experiencing the "real presence" of Jesus in eating and drinking, and if so, how does that presence relate to these elements of bread and wine?

Reflecting on John Calvin's teaching about the Lord's Supper, Martha Moore-Keish writes that "our whole selves and Christ's whole self meet one another at a communion table."[5] We come to the table as whole persons—body and soul. We are in touch with God not only through mind and memory, but through eating, drinking, and sharing with one another in the ritual action of communion. Likewise, the Christ we meet is not a figure from the distant past or abstract holiness. Rather, Calvin argued it is the Living Christ whom we meet, the One who though he was dead, is now alive and promises us the gift of new life in him.

How does this happen? Calvin's answer was that this great mystery of Christ's real presence with us in the sharing of bread and cup is the work of the Holy Spirit and the sure sign of God's unbounded love.

Notice the differences in what Jesus says in each of the Gospel accounts. How does each version add something to the meaning of the Eucharist?

Koinonia

The cup of blessing that we bless,
*   is it not a sharing in the blood of Christ?*
The bread that we break,
*   is it not a sharing in the body of Christ?*
Because there is one bread,
*   we who are many are one body, for we all partake of the one bread.*
                                        —1 Corinthians 10:16–17

"In retrospect, I can say that I joined the church out of basic need; I was becoming a Christian, and as the religion can't be practiced alone, I needed to try to align myself with a community of faith."[6] So writes Kathleen Norris about joining a small Presbyterian congregation in South Dakota, a congregation full of faith and conflict, fellowship and strife, just like the church in Corinth.

This brief passage about the Eucharist is tucked into Paul's response to a number of things the Corinthian community is arguing about. In this case, the issue is about eating food that might (or might not) have passed through the ritual slaughterhouse (and thus have been "sacrificed to idols"). The key idea here is in the word "sharing." When we share the bread, we share in the body of Christ. In Greek, the word is koinonia. It can also be translated as "participation" or "fellowship." Paul sometimes uses this word to describe how believers in one region participate in the ministry in other places. A koinonia or fellowship is what we become when we are baptized into Christ and share his body, the bread.

In the Lord's Supper, we meet the Body of Christ in two ways—in the bread we eat and in the koinonia we have with each other. One of the most significant "reforms" of Reformation was the insistence that whenever the Lord's Supper was celebrated, the entire congregation was to participate and receive both bread and cup. For several centuries in Europe, it had become the custom for only the priests to receive and for the congregation to pray silently and watch during communion.

What the Reformers reinstituted is now the norm across the Christian world. There is no communion without community because together we are the Body of Christ, and it is his life we share whenever we break bread and bless the cup.

When and how do you experience Christian community?

Breakfast on the Beach

After these things Jesus showed himself again to the disciples by the Sea of Tiberias; and he showed himself in this way. Gathered there together were Simon Peter, Thomas called the Twin, Nathanael of Cana in Galilee, the sons of Zebedee, and two others of his disciples. Simon Peter said to them, "I am going fishing."

They said to him, "We will go with you."

They went out and got into the boat, but that night they caught nothing. Just after daybreak, Jesus stood on the beach; but the disciples did not know that it was Jesus.

Jesus said to them, "Children, you have no fish, have you?"

They answered him, "No."

He said to them, "Cast the net to the right side of the boat, and you will find some."

So they cast it, and now they were not able to haul it in because there were so many fish.

That disciple whom Jesus loved said to Peter, "It is the Lord!" When Simon Peter heard that it was the Lord, he put on some clothes, for he was naked, and jumped into the sea. But the other disciples came in the boat, dragging the net full of fish, for they were not far from the land, only about a hundred yards off.

When they had gone ashore, they saw a charcoal fire there, with fish on it, and bread.

Jesus said to them, "Bring some of the fish that you have just caught."

So Simon Peter went aboard and hauled the net ashore, full of large fish, a hundred fifty-three of them; and though there were so many, the net was not torn.

Jesus said to them, "Come and have breakfast."

God's Abundant Table

Now none of the disciples dared to ask him, "Who are you?" because they knew it was the Lord. Jesus came and took the bread and gave it to them, and did the same with the fish. This was now the third time that Jesus appeared to the disciples after he was raised from the dead.

—John 21:1–14

In the early dawn, the disciples who have gone back to fishing see a man on the beach. Coming ashore with a huge catch, they then see a fire with bread and fish ready for breakfast. All is seemingly ready, but Jesus says to them, "Bring some of the fish that you have just caught." Breakfast with the Risen Christ requires that the guests do their part in supplying food.

How does bread get to the table? Seeds are planted, crops are tended, grain is harvested, flour is milled, bread is baked, and there are many hands along the way of this process. This simple miracle of food production may have been one of the first acts of human "civilization" as hunter-gatherers became settled farmers. Bread is simultaneously the gift of nature's abundance and the work of human hands.

In order for the church to celebrate the Lord's Supper, someone or some group prepares the elements. Maybe someone purchases wafers made by a religious community. Maybe someone bakes bread and brings it. Maybe someone goes to the store, buys loaves of bread and cuts it into bite-sized pieces. As with all meals, there is preparation and cleanup, simple actions but necessary to any act of hospitality.

The disciples are at loose ends. Who wouldn't be after the astonishing events of Jesus' horrible death and astonishing resurrection? They know they are not ready for whatever is next, so they go back to what they know. And it is just there that Jesus meets them—where they live and work. After a night of hard work, he knows what they need—breakfast.

This story reminds us that this is where we should be prepared to meet God: not only in church but at work, in the midst of everyday life; not only in the beauty of praise and worship but at the dinner table where hungry bodies are fed and satisfied. And it reminds us that both at the Lord's Table and in our everyday meetings, God invites us to bring bread that God will transform into God's own presence among us.

Feed Them

When they had finished breakfast, Jesus said to Simon Peter, "Simon son of John, do you love me more than these?"

He said to him, "Yes, Lord; you know that I love you."

Jesus said to him, "Feed my lambs."

A second time he said to him, "Simon son of John, do you love me?"

He said to him, "Yes, Lord; you know that I love you."

Jesus said to him, "Tend my sheep."

He said to him the third time, "Simon son of John, do you love me?"

Peter felt hurt because he said to him the third time, "Do you love me?" And he said to him, "Lord, you know everything; you know that I love you."

Jesus said to him, "Feed my sheep. Very truly, I tell you, when you were younger, you used to fasten your own belt and to go wherever you wished. But when you grow old, you will stretch out your hands, and someone else will fasten a belt around you and take you where you do not wish to go." (He said this to indicate the kind of death by which he would glorify God.)

After this he said to him, "Follow me."

—John 21:15–19

Having been fed by Jesus, the next step for the disciples is very simple: feed my sheep. This poignant story of Jesus' three-fold question to Peter is widely read as a "reversal" of Peter's three-fold denial of Jesus. It is also generally read metaphorically: feeding is a metaphor for pastoral care and oversight. This is what pastors do—they feed the flock entrusted to their care by preaching, teaching, visiting the sick and dying, binding up the broken-hearted, and so on.

But what if you read or hear this passage literally, as Sara Miles did. Her conversion began the day she wandered into an Episcopal church in San Francisco and "ate Jesus." It took root as she created a food pantry to feed people the way Jesus had fed her. It deepened as she was drawn to finding ways to feed people who were too poor even to make it out of their neighborhood to the church and the pantry.

The work was not easy. People waiting for food jockeyed for space and sometimes argued, church members worried about damage to the church building, and taking food into housing projects came with its own set of dangers. But all of it became the occasion through which Miles met God in the lives of those she worked with and those she served.

The model for the pantry was Jesus' radical hospitality—whoever came was fed. One day, at the main food bank, she was exclaiming over the dramatic increase in numbers of people showing up to get help. The manager/food distributer said, "You know about double-dipping. Lots of folks go to more than one pantry. You don't check ID, right?"

"I know," I said wearily. . . . "I mean, feed my sheep. You know what I'm saying?"

"I know," said Eddie in a different tone. . . .
"Feed my sheep, feed my sheep," I repeated. "He didn't say 'Feed my sheep after you check their ID.' " . . .

"Okay," Eddie said. "Don't worry, sister, we'll get you more food."[7]

How is feeding hungry people an act of prayer?

Chapter 5

Giving Thanks

Eucharist

Bless the LORD, O my soul,
and all that is within me, bless his holy name.
Bless the LORD, O my soul,
and do not forget all his benefits—
who forgives all your iniquity,
who heals all your diseases,
who redeems your life from the Pit,
who crowns you with steadfast love and mercy,
who satisfies you with good as long as you live
so that your youth is renewed like the eagle's.

The LORD works vindication
and justice for all who are oppressed.
He made known his ways to Moses,
his acts to the people of Israel.
The LORD is merciful and gracious,
slow to anger and abounding in steadfast love.
He will not always accuse,
nor will he keep his anger forever.
He does not deal with us according to our sins,
nor repay us according to our iniquities.
For as the heavens are high above the earth,
so great is his steadfast love toward those who fear him;
as far as the east is from the west,
so far he removes our transgressions from us.
As a father has compassion for his children,
so the LORD has compassion for those who fear him.
For he knows how we were made;
he remembers that we are dust.

—Psalm 103:1–14

The Lord's Supper is called by many names, but the most ancient are "the Lord's supper" (1 Corinthians 11:20), the "breaking of bread" (Acts 2:42 and 46), and the "Eucharist" (*Didache*, IX.1).[8] The name "Eucharist" is the Greek word that means "thanksgiving." For the earliest church, the meal shared in the Spirit of Jesus was above all an act of gratitude and great joy.

On one level, this act of giving thanks before sharing bread and cup repeats what Jesus himself was recorded to have done. And his action in turn is what any devout Jew would have done at any meal—saying a blessing over bread that gave God thanks and praise for the gift of food: "Blessed are you, O Lord our God, King of the universe. You bring forth bread from the earth."[9]

On another level, the ritual act of giving thanks came to define the meal itself. Sharing bread and cup in the Spirit of Jesus became the occasion to give thanks for everything that God had done, and the prayer became a recital of the "mighty acts of God" culminating in what God had done through the life and ministry, the death and resurrection of Jesus.

In this way, the Lord's Supper continues the prayer practice of the Temple psalms, which recite the goodness and mercy that God has shown down through the ages to God's people, Israel. Jesus learned these songs as a child. Jews and Christians have sung and read them for centuries. Just as parents teach children when and how to say "please" and "thank you," so the psalms teach God's people how to give thanks. We learn to praise God for the goodness and beauty of creation, for God's act of freeing Israel from slavery, for the amazing gift of the Law by which Israel could learn how to walk with God, for healing, for forgiveness, for mercy, for life.

For what are you most grateful? How often do you take time to stop and give thanks?

Great Prayer of Thanksgiving

Blessed are you, strong and faithful God.
All your works, the height and the depth,
echo the silent music of your praise.
In the beginning your Word summoned light,
night withdrew, and creation dawned.

God's Abundant Table

As ages passed unseen,
waters gathered on the face of the earth
and life appeared.
When the times at last had ripened
and the earth grown full in abundance,
you created in your image man and woman,
the stewards of all creation.
You gave us breath and speech,
that all the living
might find a voice to sing your praise,
and to celebrate the creation you call good.
So now, with all the powers of heaven and earth,
we sing the ageless hymn of your glory:

Holy, holy, holy Lord, God of power and might,
heaven and earth are full of your glory.
Hosanna in the highest.
Blessed is he who comes in the name of the Lord.
Hosanna in the highest.[10]

— International Committee
on English in the Liturgy

The prayer that is offered as the church gathers at the Lord's Table is at the same time an act of grateful joy and an affirmation of the core of Christian faith. In this prayer, we give thanks as we recite the story of what God has done with and for us and all creation. In keeping with our belief in the triune God, the Great Thanksgiving is a prayer in three parts. The first section (often called the preface) addresses God as Creator or Father. Sometimes the prayer focuses as it does here on God's work of creation; some prayers lift up the theme of God's covenant promises with Israel; some prayers lift up the season of the liturgical year or a specific celebration or observance as thanks and praise are offered.

The ways in which we can give voice to our gratitude are as limitless as the goodness and grace that God shows to us.

Notice how this particular preface tells the story of creation, combining the sequence of Genesis 1 with the scientific evidence that the earth and life have taken their current shape over many millions of years. This prayer also lifts up the distinctive vocation of humanity: to be "stewards" of creation and also to be the creatures that are able to give voice to the praise that the rest of creation offers silently. Finally, this exuberant prayer reminds us that creation and redemption are not two different things for both stem from the same source—the unbounded love of God.

What would you add to a prayer of thanksgiving for God's goodness?

Remembering

All holy God,
how wonderful is the work of your hands!
When sin had scarred the world,
you entered into covenant to renew the whole creation.
As a mother tenderly gathers her children,
as a father joyfully welcomes his own,
you embraced a people as your own
and filled them with longing
for a peace that would last
and for a justice that would never fail.
Through countless generations
your people hungered for the bread of freedom.
From them you raised up Jesus, your Son,
the living bread, in whom ancient hungers are satisfied.
He healed the sick,
though he himself would suffer;
he offered life to sinners,
though death would hunt him down.
But with a love stronger than death,
he opened wide his arms
and surrendered his spirit.

God's Abundant Table

Gracious God,
as we offer you our sacrifice of praise and thanksgiving,
we commemorate Jesus, your Son.
Death could not bind him,
for you raised him up in the Spirit of holiness
and exalted him as Lord of creation.

Great is the mystery of faith:
Christ has died,
Christ is risen,
Christ will come again.[11]

—International Committee
on English in the Liturgy

The second part of the Great Thanksgiving is often called the "anamnesis," from a Greek word that means "remembrance." In this section, the focus is on Jesus, but the "memory" we lift up goes beyond the "last supper" in the Upper Room. The saving work of Christ encompasses far more than his sacrifice on the cross. It is Jesus' entire life and ministry that demonstrate the nature of divine love, the love that is fulfilled in Jesus' willingness to lay down his life for his friends. This love is stronger than death, and leads us to the joyful affirmation that Christ *has* died in the past; he *is risen* now; he *will come again* to usher in the fullness of God's reign.

In this version of the remembrance of Jesus, the prayer lifts up his place in the long line of God's redeeming activity. God began the story of redemption with the covenant with Abraham, through whom God promised to bless all humanity. Jesus, the one in whom the fullness of God lived among us, is the culmination of God's long-standing desire to restore creation and renew human life in right relationship with God. As such, he is the source of our hope for abundant and everlasting life.

How would you tell the story of Jesus? Which events are most important to lift up in a prayer of thanksgiving?

Invoking the Spirit

Eternal God,
let your Holy Spirit move in power over us
and over these earthly gifts of bread and wine,
that they may be the communion of the body and blood of Christ,
and that we may become one in him.
May his coming in glory find us
ever watchful in prayer,
strong in truth and love,
and faithful in the breaking of the bread.
Then, at last, all peoples will be free,
all divisions healed,
and with your whole creation,
we will sing your praise,
through your Son, Jesus Christ.
Through Christ, with Christ, in Christ,
in the unity of the Holy Spirit,
all glory and honor are yours, almighty Father,
*forever and ever. **Amen.***[12]

— International Committee on English in the Liturgy

The third section of the Great Thanksgiving is often called the "epiclesis" or "calling forth" because here the prayer invokes God the Holy Spirit to be present and bless the elements of bread and wine and the congregation gathered at the Lord's Table. Christians have argued for centuries about what happens at this point. Do the elements change in some way? Do bread and wine "become" the body and blood of Christ? John Calvin argued that, although the physical substance of bread and wine remains the same, the Holy Spirit invoked in this prayer makes Christ *really present* to believers as they partake. In the same way, Calvin taught, the Holy Spirit makes the words of the Bible *become* the Word of God for us. This is the purpose of the Prayer for Illumination before the reading of Scripture and the sermon in worship.

The Spirit not only makes Christ present to us; the Spirit makes us one with each other and one with Christ as we eat and drink together.

God's Abundant Table

Just as the Spirit moved over the face of the deep at creation, so the Spirit makes us a new community, new people in Christ.

Notice as well how this prayer looks forward, not backward, in time. The Spirit gives us courage to wait actively and faithfully for the return of Christ and the fulfillment of God's promises. In this particular prayer, notice how the description of the future—when all people are free, all divisions healed, and the whole creation joins in praise—picks up the themes of the first two sections of the prayer, which celebrated the goodness of creation and the longing of humanity for freedom, wholeness, and peace.

What does it mean to wait in hope for the fulfillment of the reign of God?

The Eyes of All Look to You

I will extol you, my God and King,
*   and bless your name forever and ever.*
Every day I will bless you,
*   and praise your name forever and ever.*
Great is the LORD, and greatly to be praised;
*   his greatness is unsearchable.*

One generation shall laud your works to another,
*   and shall declare your mighty acts.*
On the glorious splendor of your majesty,
*   and on your wondrous works, I will meditate.*
The might of your awesome deeds shall be proclaimed,
*   and I will declare your greatness.*
They shall celebrate the fame of your abundant goodness,
*   and shall sing aloud of your righteousness.*

The LORD is gracious and merciful,
*   slow to anger and abounding in steadfast love.*
The LORD is good to all,
*   and his compassion is over all that he has made.*

All your works shall give thanks to you, O Lord,
   and all your faithful shall bless you.
They shall speak of the glory of your kingdom,
   and tell of your power,
to make known to all people your mighty deeds,
   and the glorious splendor of your kingdom.
Your kingdom is an everlasting kingdom,
   and your dominion endures throughout all generations.

The Lord is faithful in all his words,
   and gracious in all his deeds.
The Lord upholds all who are falling,
   and raises up all who are bowed down.
The eyes of all look to you,
   and you give them their food in due season.
You open your hand,
   satisfying the desire of every living thing.
The Lord is just in all his ways,
   and kind in all his doings.
The Lord is near to all who call on him,
   to all who call on him in truth.
He fulfills the desire of all who fear him;
   he also hears their cry, and saves them.
The Lord watches over all who love him,
   but all the wicked he will destroy.
My mouth will speak the praise of the Lord,
   and all flesh will bless his holy name forever and ever.
                                        —Psalm 145

In the one hymn attributed to John Calvin, we find these lovely lines: "Thou art the life, by which alone we live, And all our substance and our strength receive. . . "[13] As far as we know, Calvin did not write this based on Psalm 145, but the themes are clearly similar. In this magnificent prayer, the psalmist finds multiple ways to express the goodness and the generosity of God. God is "gracious and merciful, slow to anger and abounding in steadfast love." God is compassionate to all; humans and animals alike look to God for sustenance: "The eyes of all look to you, and you give them their food in due season. You open your hand, satisfying the desire of every living thing."

One of Calvin's favorite metaphors for God's goodness was a fountain. Just as water from a large fountain in the middle of a city park rises up into the air and cascades down into a pool providing cooling mists and delightful sounds, so too the goodness of God is an inexhaustible stream cascading through creation. It is the very source of life itself.

The problem, as Calvin saw it, is that the crippling effect of human sin has blinded us to the goodness of God. We can no longer see the beauty and abundance of God's mercy in everything around us and within our own hearts and lives. To shift the metaphor slightly, it is as though construction barriers or barricades blocked off the fountain. We might still get a glimpse of the water or hear its sound faintly, but we can no longer get close to the life-giving water itself.

This is where Christ enters the picture. Christ's role is to open the way to the fountain, to lead us back so that we can once again see, feel, touch, hear, and taste the goodness of God on display around and within. As we hear the Word and taste the bread and wine, we are fed—both body and soul—by the living Christ.

Where do you see the goodness of God in your everyday experience? How many examples can you find in one day?

Grateful

When you have come into the land that the LORD your God is giving you as an inheritance to possess, and you possess it, and settle in it, you shall take some of the first of all the fruit of the ground, which you harvest from the land that the LORD your God is giving you, and you shall put it in a basket and go to the place that the LORD your God will choose as a dwelling for his name. You shall go to the priest who is in office at that time, and say to him, "Today I declare to the LORD your God that I have come into the land that the LORD swore to our ancestors to give us."

When the priest takes the basket from your hand and sets it down before the altar of the LORD your God, you shall make this response before the LORD your God: "A wandering Aramean was my ancestor; he went down into Egypt and lived there as an alien, few in number, and there he became a great nation, mighty and populous. When the Egyptians treated us harshly and afflicted us, by imposing hard labor on us, we cried to the LORD, the God of our ancestors; the LORD heard our voice and saw our affliction, our toil, and our oppression. The LORD brought us out of Egypt with a mighty hand and an outstretched arm, with a terrifying display of power, and with signs and wonders; and he brought us into this place and gave us this land, a land flowing with milk and honey. So now I bring the first of the fruit of the ground that you, O LORD, have given me."

You shall set it down before the LORD your God and bow down before the LORD your God. Then you, together with the Levites and the aliens who reside among you, shall celebrate with all the bounty that the LORD your God has given to you and to your house.

—Deuteronomy 26:1–11

What do you do when you become convinced of God's generosity? What do you do when your life is filled with abundance? The liturgy described in Deuteronomy 26 is the answer. Those who know their lives to be filled with God's goodness are to respond in kind. In the words of theologian Brian Gerrish, grace leads to gratitude.[14]

In this text, we are to imagine Israel now settled in the land God has promised. No longer wandering in the wilderness, the people are now farmers and shepherds, cultivating the crops and animals that sustain life. When harvest time comes, they are to bring the "first fruits" of their labor as an offering to God. As they present these gifts before God, the people are to recite the story of how they got to the land in the first place. Scholars call this one of the first "creeds" in the Bible, but mostly it is a short version of Israel's history from Abraham through the Exodus back to the land of promise. After this act of offering, the people, the priests, and "the aliens who reside among you" join in celebration, that is to say, they have a great feast from the food offerings they have brought to God.

This liturgy of thanksgiving has four movements: the people bring their produce; they offer the items to God and the priest places them before the altar; they declare their faith or recite the reason for their gratitude; and then they celebrate—they eat together. Notice how similar these actions are to what we do in the Lord's Supper. We bring bread and wine to the Table; we offer them to God; in our prayer of thanks, we recite the reasons for our gratitude; and finally, we eat and drink together.

In the ancient story and at the Lord's Table, this offering of thanksgiving is our grateful response to God summed up in these words: "So now I bring the first of the fruit of the ground that you, O Lord, have given me."

How does your life express gratitude for what God has given you?

Treasure

Someone in the crowd said to him, "Teacher, tell my brother to divide the family inheritance with me."

But he said to him, "Friend, who set me to be a judge or arbitrator over you? And he said to them, "Take care! Be on your guard against all kinds of greed; for one's life does not consist in the abundance of possessions."

Then he told them a parable: "The land of a rich man produced abundantly. And he thought to himself, 'What should I do, for I have no place to store my crops?' Then he said, 'I will do this: I will pull down my barns and build larger ones, and there I will store all my grain and my goods. And I will say to my soul, 'Soul, you have ample goods laid up for many years; relax, eat, drink, be merry.' But God said to him, 'You fool! This very night your life is being demanded of you. And the things you have prepared, whose will they be?'

So it is with those who store up treasures for themselves but are not rich toward God."

—Luke 12:13–21

What do you do when you realize that you have more than you need? Jesus tells this parable about a rich man who has a bumper crop. He already has more than he needs, but now his land produces even more! Not having enough storage, he decides to replace his current barns with bigger ones. In other words, he decides to invest some of his profit so that he can preserve his assets. From one point of view, this seems like a perfectly reasonable thing to do. I can remember getting some extra spending money early on in life and hearing my father say: "Don't spend it all in one place!" What he actually meant was: don't spend it at all! A surplus is to be "put away for a rainy day."

So what is the problem here? The key is in the word "abundance"— the land produced abundantly! But does the farmer recognize abundance when he sees it? Obviously, he knows that he has "more" than he anticipated, but does he see it is "abundance"—an extravagant amount, so much that it could never be exhausted? No, he does not. What he sees is simply more that needs to be protected and kept for his own future use. Even though he has more than enough, his way of looking at things imagines that scarcity is more powerful than abundance.

That is not at all how Jesus sees this, as he makes clear in the teaching that follows: "Do not worry about your life, what you will eat, or about your body, what you will wear. . . . Consider the ravens: they neither sow nor reap, they have neither storehouse nor barn, and yet God feeds them" (vv. 22 and 24). God is in the abundance business, and the lavish beauty of creation is the proof of this. The problem with the so-called "rich fool" is a failure of imagination. He can't see abundance for what it is: a sign of how God relates to the world—as a generous giver. He can't see that his response to abundance should mimic God's—he should just give it away!

You have more than you need; what are you doing with it?

Chapter 6

A Drama in Five Acts

Do This in Remembrance

For I received from the Lord what I also handed on to you, that the Lord Jesus on the night when he was betrayed took a loaf of bread, and when he had given thanks, he broke it and said, "This is my body that is for you. Do this in remembrance of me." In the same way he took the cup also, after supper, saying, "This cup is the new covenant in my blood. Do this, as often as you drink it, in remembrance of me."

—1 Corinthians 11:23–25

For most of the church's life, understanding the Eucharist has focused on the first sentence in the Words of Institution: "This is my body." Theologians and teachers of the faith have argued about how the bread is or isn't Jesus' body and when it changes, if it does. That is to say, much of the church's reflection has focused on the elements themselves.

But what if the important sentence is the second: "Do this in remembrance of me." When this sentence is highlighted, most of the discussion has centered on the word "remembrance." What does it mean to "remember" and what precisely are we to "remember"? When this becomes the focus, scholars and teachers have shifted the focus from the elements (bread and wine) to us—to something that goes on in our minds or spirits. It is, after all, we who are doing the remembering. And remembering is fundamentally a private or personal act.

Another angle of vision is to focus instead on the word "do:" "Do this in remembrance of me." What are we doing? We are gathering as the community that follows Jesus; we are praying; we are sharing bread and wine together. Now the focus is not on individual believers but on the community gathered, because the meal is a group activity. The community engages together in a ritual act that involves speaking, moving around, eating, drinking, and maybe singing. It is like a drama in which the story of God's great love for us is reenacted and experienced.

Take Bread

And taking the five loaves and the two fish, he looked up to heaven, and blessed and broke them, and gave them to the disciples to set before the crowd. And all ate and were filled. What was left over was gathered up, twelve baskets of broken pieces.

Then he took a loaf of bread, and when he had given thanks, he broke it and gave it to them, saying, "This is my body, which is given for you. Do this in remembrance of me."

When he was at the table with them, he took bread, blessed and broke it, and gave it to them. Then their eyes were opened, and they recognized him; and he vanished from their sight.

—Luke 9:16–17, 22:19; 24:30–31

Dom Gregory Dix, noted liturgical and biblical scholar, wrote that the Eucharist is made up of four actions illustrated in these texts (and in all the other versions of the loaves and fishes and the Upper Room stories). This deliberate repetition led Dix to conclude that by the time the Gospels were written (two generations after Jesus' resurrection) these actions reflected what the church was already doing during worship. In each account, Jesus took bread, gave thanks (or blessed God for it), broke the bread, and gave it to those he was eating with. To take, to give thanks, to break, and to give: these actions (along with the words) make the meal a Eucharist—a meal in the Spirit with Jesus.

What does it mean to take the bread? This action reminds us that the bread Jesus used, like the bread we use in worship and on our everyday tables, comes from somewhere else. Jesus did not make bread appear magically (or make it out of stones, as the Tempter suggested). Jesus took the bread that someone had given him. That person, in turn, either made the bread or bought the bread from the one who made it. That person began with flour that had been milled from grain that yet another person planted, tended, and harvested. Ultimately, grain is the result of the organic process of seeds germinating, growing, and maturing.

Before there can be a Eucharist, the work of many people is required. Before there can be a meal of any kind, human agency and the processes of nature must be combined to produce food. Especially for those who live in urban areas, the meals we prepare and eat represent the final stage in a process of food production that involves many people often at great distances from us. Many of those people along the way work for very low wages and may themselves not have enough to eat. Whenever we take food, prayer should be offered for the many hands that brought it and for the earth itself.

Where does the food you eat come from?

Bless God

> As for mortals, their days are like grass;
>   they flourish like a flower of the field;
> for the wind passes over it, and it is gone,
>   and its place knows it no more.
> But the steadfast love of the LORD is from everlasting to everlasting
>   on those who fear him,
>   and his righteousness to children's children,
>   to those who keep his covenant and remember to do his
>   commandments.
> The LORD has established his throne in the heavens,
>   and his kingdom rules over all.
> Bless the LORD, O you his angels,
>   you mighty ones who do his bidding, obedient to his spoken word.
> Bless the LORD, all his hosts,
>   his ministers that do his will.
> Bless the LORD, all his works,
>   in all places of his dominion.
> Bless the LORD, O my soul.

—Psalm 103:15–22

What do you give the One who has given everything? Israel's faith suggests that the appropriate responses are thanksgiving, praise, and blessing. "Bless the LORD, O my soul, and do not forget all [God's] benefits." The idea of blessing goes back to the beginning of the biblical story, as God blesses the first humans (Genesis 1:28) and commissions them to care for the earth. Later, we see parents blessing their children (and Jacob cheating his brother Esau out of Isaac's blessing). When God blesses particular individuals, it is in the context of making covenants: God blesses Noah after the flood, making a covenant promise never again to destroy life; later, God blesses Abraham, promising that "in you all the families of the earth shall be blessed" (Genesis 12:3).

The act of blessing defines the relationship between God and humankind. It is "the circle in which God connects with the community and the community connects with God."[15] When we bless or are blessed by another person, the action acknowledges and enacts a deep bond of relationship. In Jewish homes, it is customary before the Sabbath meal for parents to bless their children—an intimate act of love and care. The blessing a pastor gives at the end of a worship service is a prayer that all present will carry from that service the peace and presence that God has given them during worship.

When we bless God for bread and bless the bread, we acknowledge that the bread symbolizes everything we need to sustain life and that all of this comes to us from God. In so doing, we confirm that we understand ourselves to be standing in relationship to God, and that this relationship is what gives us life, wholeness, and peace.

As God has blessed us, so we bless the Lord. The circle of life goes on.

How has God blessed you? How do you bless the Lord?

Break Bread

Jesus answered them, "The hour has come for the Son of Man to be glorified. Very truly, I tell you, unless a grain of wheat falls into the earth and dies, it remains just a single grain; but if it dies, it bears much fruit. Those who love their life lose it, and those who hate their life in this world will keep it for eternal life. Whoever serves me must follow me, and where I am, there will my servant be also. Whoever serves me, the Father will honor."

Then he poured water into a basin and began to wash the disciples' feet and to wipe them with the towel that was tied around him. He came to Simon Peter, who said to him, "Lord, are you going to wash my feet?"

Jesus answered, "You do not know now what I am doing, but later you will understand."

Peter said to him, "You will never wash my feet."
Jesus answered, "Unless I wash you, you have no share with me."

—John 12:23–26; 13:5–8

What is the difference between a loaf of bread and a dinner roll? The dinner roll is an individual portion, meant to serve only one person. A loaf of bread is meant to serve many people; it is designed to be shared, and in order to be shared it must first be broken.

This is the third of the "acts" that makes a Eucharist—just as Jesus broke the bread, so when celebrating the Eucharist, the minister breaks a loaf (or cracker or wafer) while repeating the Words of Institution. The breaking of the loaf is practical—it is the way the bread is divided so that everyone at the table gets some. This is the foundation for the first symbolic meaning: we who share a common loaf of bread have a new relationship with one another—we become (even if only during this meal) "companions," those who are together "with bread." Since the bread that we share at the Lord's Table is the Body of Christ, then we who share it come into a new relationship with Christ as well as with one another. When we eat with Christ, we come to have a "share" in him, as Jesus says in relationship to the foot-washing in the Upper Room.

There is another layer of symbolism in broken bread, of course, and that is the reminder that Jesus' own body was "broken" and his life poured out. Why was it necessary for Jesus to be put to death? How does his death reconcile us to God? The Bible and great teachers of the faith have struggled over the centuries to find adequate ways to answer these questions.[16] Finally, this is a deep mystery that displays the lengths to which love is willing to go to call us home.

That love is what we are invited to take into ourselves whenever we eat the broken bread as we say to each other, "the Body of Christ broken for you."

What comes to mind as you reflect on the words "This is my body broken for you"?

Give

The apostles gathered around Jesus, and told him all that they had done and taught. He said to them, "Come away to a deserted place all by yourselves and rest a while."

For many were coming and going, and they had no leisure even to eat. And they went away in the boat to a deserted place by themselves. Now many saw them going and recognized them, and they hurried there on foot from all the towns and arrived ahead of them.

As he went ashore, he saw a great crowd; and he had compassion for them, because they were like sheep without a shepherd; and he began to teach them many things.

When it grew late, his disciples came to him and said, "This is a deserted place, and the hour is now very late; send them away so that they may go into the surrounding country and villages and buy something for themselves to eat."

But he answered them, "You give them something to eat." They said to him, "Are we to go and buy two hundred denarii worth of bread, and give it to them to eat?"

And he said to them, "How many loaves have you? Go and see." When they had found out, they said, "Five, and two fish."

Then he ordered them to get all the people to sit down in groups on the green grass. So they sat down in groups of hundreds and of fifties. Taking the five loaves and the two fish, he looked up to heaven, and blessed and broke the loaves, and gave them to his disciples to set before the people; and he divided the two fish among them all. And all ate and were filled; and they took up twelve baskets full of broken pieces and of the fish. Those who had eaten the loaves numbered five thousand men.

—Mark 6:30–44

Why did Jesus not serve the crowd himself? Why make such a point of this fourth move? What is the significance of the fourth "act" of the Eucharist—what does it mean to *give?*

In the feeding stories, it seems obvious. Even allowing for biblical exaggeration of numbers, a lot of people need to be fed. In this version, Jesus instructs the crowd to organize themselves into groups of fifties and hundreds (which may reflect the way Moses divided the people of Israel in the wilderness; see Exodus 18:25) to facilitate serving.

On another level, this action symbolizes the essence of ministry. Mark places this feeding story immediately after the disciples return from their first "preaching mission" (6:6b–13). When they come home from the amazing experience of casting out demons and curing the sick, the very next thing Jesus asks them to do is serve bread and fish to hungry people. Jesus' disciples are and will be leaders, but this simple story reminded them—and reminds us—that Christian leadership is shaped by service. Those who would be "in charge" are also going to do setup and cleanup.

When Presbyterians celebrate the Eucharist, this is vividly on display. The role of the Minister of Word and Sacrament is to lead the community in prayer. The role of the elders and deacons is to serve the people—to distribute the bread and cup. One congregation makes this clear in the liturgy itself. After the Words of Institution, the pastor says, "Ministering in His name, we bring this bread and cup to you."

Just as Jesus did not do all the work of ministry himself but called disciples to work with and alongside him during his earthly life, so today he calls women and men to serve in his name, to stand in his place, to bring food to the hungry, hope to the despairing, light in the darkness.

Think about distributing bread as a model for leadership. What does that suggest to you?

Fasting

Is not this the fast that I choose:
*   to loose the bonds of injustice,*
*   to undo the thongs of the yoke,*
to let the oppressed go free,
*   and to break every yoke?*
Is it not to share your bread with the hungry,
*   and bring the homeless poor into your house;*
when you see the naked, to cover them,
*   and not to hide yourself from your own kin?*
Then your light shall break forth like the dawn,
*   and your healing shall spring up quickly;*
your vindicator shall go before you,
*   the glory of the LORD shall be your rear guard.*
Then you shall call, and the LORD will answer;
*   you shall cry for help, and he will say, Here I am.*
If you remove the yoke from among you,
*   the pointing of the finger, the speaking of evil,*
if you offer your food to the hungry
*   and satisfy the needs of the afflicted,*
then your light shall rise in the darkness
*   and your gloom be like the noonday.*
*   —Isaiah 58:6–10*

For many religious traditions, including ancient Israel and modern Judaism, fasting is an important prayer practice. It is often seen as an act of purification or a time to focus on God. In this passage, the people seem to have been observing a fast but not having the experience of forgiveness or renewal or drawing closer to God. The problem is that the act of fasting has not been accompanied by acts of justice; deeds of mercy have not been offered along with prayer. Prayer that has no concern for those without food, clothing, and shelter is not prayer— or at least not the kind of prayer that the God of Israel desires.

In the early church, it was often the custom when the Eucharist was celebrated to take the bread from the table out to those of the community who could not be present (either because they were too sick to join the community or because they had to work when the community gathered). Then the leftover bread was distributed to the poor both within and beyond the community.

The four "acts" of the Eucharist are completed by a fifth: to *share*. The bread that God gives is meant not only for the soul but for the body. God fed Israel manna in the wilderness. It was bread from heaven, but the purpose was to keep them alive. Jesus multiplied the loaves and fishes, but the point was that they were hungry.

Christian worship is centered on receiving bread from the Lord's Table. As we receive God's grace in Jesus Christ, we offer God our thanks and praise. The words of the prophet Isaiah and the actions of Jesus remind us that our prayers will find their appropriate fulfillment when we share what we have received with those in need. Being well-fed at the Lord's Table requires us to feed the hungry—with the good news of God's love and with real bread.

How does your congregation share the bread of life both as the good news and as real food?

God's Abundant Table

They devoted themselves to the apostles' teaching and fellowship, to the breaking of bread and the prayers. Awe came upon everyone, because many wonders and signs were being done by the apostles. All who believed were together and had all things in common; they would sell their possessions and goods and distribute the proceeds to all, as any had need. Day by day, as they spent much time together in the temple, they broke bread at home and ate their food with glad and generous hearts, praising God and having the goodwill of all the people.

—Acts 2:42–47a

Now to Your table spread
We come, each one in faith
That You alone provide the words of life and death:
In wine and bread, In promised food
We find Your loving heart, O God.

Hands of the world stretch out
Your mystery to touch
In longing to believe a truth beyond our reach,
To sing in joy, To cry in grief,
To know Your meaning for our life.

Here is our common wealth
In sharing what is good,
As though all humankind around one table stood,
This bread to break, This wine to taste:
One people in the name of Christ.[17]
　　　　　　　—Shirley Erena Murray (1987)

Sessions for Group Study

SESSION 1

Bread Everywhere

MAIN IDEA

The Lord's Supper or Eucharist is "the joyful feast of the people of God." The readings suggest how it is connected to other feasts in the biblical story and to our own experience of feasting and celebration.

PREPARING TO LEAD

- Read chapter 1.
- Read this session and select questions and activities that you will use. What other questions, issues, or themes occur to you from your reflection?
- Each session includes a hymn. If you do not have a piano or keyboard and someone to play, consider asking someone to record the music so that the group can sing the hymn. Many prayers in worship will be taken from the *Book of Common Worship*, in particular from the "Great Thanksgiving" prayers. You may want to have a copy and review the sources.
- The central theme of this study is that the Lord's Supper is more than a "remembrance" of the Last Supper. When we celebrate the Eucharist (another name for the Lord's Supper, which comes from the Greek and means "thanksgiving"), we are invited to remember the many other feasts in the biblical story and recall how God has always fed God's people. We are also to look forward into the future as this feast is also a symbol of the kingdom or reign of God at the end of time.
- Finally, experiencing the Lord's Supper as a feast invites us to reflect on our own experiences of feasting and celebration. This works both ways: our experiences with food and feasting affect how we experience the Eucharist, and our understanding of the Eucharist as "joyful feast" can inform our ordinary practices of feasting and sharing food.

GATHERING

- If this is a newly formed group, provide nametags and pens as people arrive.
- Provide simple refreshments; ask a volunteer to bring refreshments next session.
- Since this is the first session, agree on simple "ground rules" and logistics (for example, time to begin and end; location for meetings; welcoming all points of view; confidentiality; and so forth). Encourage participants to bring study book and Bibles.

OPENING WORSHIP

Prayer (*unison*)

God of all goodness, you are the source of life itself and you sustain all creation through your mercy. We thank you for feeding us each day: for food that nourishes our bodies and for your Word that feeds our spirit. Be present to us today that we may find in you the nourishment that gives us strength and courage and hope; through Jesus Christ our Lord. Amen.

Lectio Divina (*reflective or prayerful reading*)

Read Isaiah 25:6–10a aloud. Invite all to reflect for a few minutes in silence.

After reflection time, invite all to listen for a word or phrase as the passage is read again and reflect on that word or phrase in silence. Read the passage a third time, asking all to offer a silent prayer after the reading.

Invite all who wish to share the word or phrase that spoke most deeply to them.

Prayer

Loving God, you promise a future that is like an abundant and joyful feast. Hear our prayers today as we look forward to the fullness of your reign: (spoken prayers may be offered).

We thank you that you hear all the prayers of our hearts, spoken and silent. Hear us now as we pray together as Jesus taught us, saying, Our Father . . .

CONVERSATION

- Invite each member of the group briefly to share a "feast story," a "memorable meal," or celebration: who was there? What made it special? After all who want to have shared, reflect on common themes or characteristics from these stories.
- The story of the manna in the wilderness is one of the most significant images of God's provision for Israel. Why is it so memorable? What were some of your reflections on that story? What does it tell us about God?
- Review John 2:1–11. This story occurs only in John's Gospel and it has a prominent place at the very beginning of Jesus' ministry. Share reflections on the meanings of this story, remembering that in this Gospel in particular, many stories have both a literal and symbolic level of meaning.
- Invite the group to reflect on the way the Lord's Supper or Eucharist is celebrated in your congregation(s). What is the "tone" of the service? What type of music is used? Does the way the sacrament is celebrated vary during the year (for example, World Communion Sunday, All Saints' Day, Christmas, Maundy Thursday, and Easter Vigil)? Have you participated in Eucharist celebrations in other settings, other congregations or other denominations? What was different?

CONCLUSION

Prayer

The Lord be with you.
And also with you.
Lift up your hearts.
We lift them to the Lord.
Let us give thanks to the Lord our God.
It is right to give our thanks and praise.
Holy God,
Father Almighty, Creator of heaven and earth,
with joy we praise you and give thanks to your name.
You formed the universe in your wisdom,
and created all things by your power.
You set us in families on the earth to live with you in faith.

We praise you for good gifts of bread and wine,
and for the table you spread in the world
as a sign of your love for all people.
Great and wonderful are your works,
Lord God almighty.
All your ways are just and true.
Therefore we lift our hearts in joyful praise,
now and forever.
Amen.

Hymn: "Let Us Talents and Tongues Employ" (*Presbyterian Hymnal*, no. 514)

God's Abundant Table

SESSION 2

Hospitality

MAIN IDEA

Hospitality is the welcoming of others into one's life or home or congregation or community. All of us have received God's welcome in baptism. The readings for this week urge us to reflect on what it means to extend hospitality to others in our personal lives as well as in the larger society.

PREPARING TO LEAD

- Read chapter 2.
- Read this session and select questions and activities that you will use. What other questions, issues, or themes occur to you from your reflection?
- Each session includes a hymn. If you do not have a piano or keyboard and someone to play, consider asking someone to record the music so that the group can sing the hymn. Many prayers in worship will be taken from the *Book of Common Worship*, in particular from the "Great Thanksgiving" prayers. You may want to have a copy and review the sources.
- At the Lord's Table, all of us are guests, present because God in Jesus Christ has invited us; no one can claim to come to the Table because of some "entitlement." The gospel suggests that we are to treat others as God in Christ has treated us. In other words, one way to describe sharing the good news is extending "radical hospitality." By reflecting on various biblical stories about hospitality, we are invited to explore the implications of such hospitality in our personal discipleship, in our congregational life, and in terms of how our larger society operates. The idea that there is a connection between the Eucharist and social justice may be unfamiliar or unsettling. Encourage the group to explore this.

GATHERING

- Provide nametags and pens as people arrive.
- Enjoy refreshments; ask for a volunteer to bring refreshments next week.
- Review "ground rules" and logistics (for example, time to begin and end session; location for meetings; welcoming all points of view; confidentiality; and so on). Encourage participants to bring study book and Bibles.

OPENING WORSHIP

Prayer

God of grace, you are always more ready to bestow your good gifts upon us than we are to seek them. You are more willing to give than we desire or deserve. Help us to learn from your example of hospitality and generosity, that our hearts may be open to others as you have opened your heart to us in Jesus Christ our Savior. Amen.

Lectio Divina (*reflective or prayerful reading*)

Read Luke 14:12–14 aloud. Invite all to reflect for a few minutes in silence.

After reflection time, invite all to listen for a word or phrase as the passage is read again and reflect on that word or phrase in silence.

Read the passage a third time, asking all to offer a silent prayer after the reading.

Invite all who wish to share the word or phrase that spoke most deeply to them.

Prayer

Loving God, you welcome us into your family and call us to extend hospitality to others. Hear our prayers today as we pray for ourselves and your world: (spoken prayers may be offered).

We thank you that you hear all the prayers of our hearts, spoken and silent. Hear us now as we pray together as Jesus taught us, saying, Our Father . . .

CONVERSATION

- Invite the group to share what "hospitality" meant in the family or community in which they grew up. Note that what constitutes hospitality and how it is demonstrated differs by culture and context. If members of the group have lived outside the United States or traveled extensively, invite them to share experiences of hospitality in other cultures.
- In two of the readings for this week, Jesus is the guest of others (Luke 10; 14). In both cases, he teaches others about hospitality. What does he teach?
- There are always limits on hospitality; we don't invite just anyone or everyone into our homes and lives. And yet we are called to welcome others as God in Christ has welcomed us. How does the gospel challenge the limits we place on hospitality? What do you make of the idea in the reflection on Mark 7:24–30 that even Jesus could be challenged with the limits on his own sense of hospitality?
- How welcoming or hospitable is your congregation? How easy is it for a visitor or newcomer to feel welcome? Are there unwritten rules for membership or inclusion?
- Reflect on Elam Davies' call for the church to reach out to "the least, the last, the lost, and the left-behind." Who are those people in your community? What is your congregation doing with and for them?
- Immigration policy is a major issue in the United States and other countries today. What does a gospel of hospitality have to do with issues such as immigration and the treatment of undocumented persons?

CONCLUSION

Prayer

The Lord be with you.
And also with you.
Lift up your hearts.
We lift them to the Lord.
Let us give thanks to the Lord our God.
It is right to give our thanks and praise.

We bless you for creating the whole world, for your promises to your
people Israel, and for Jesus Christ in whom your fullness dwells.
Born of Mary, he shares our life.
Eating with sinners, he welcomes us.
Guiding his children, he leads us.
Visiting the sick, he heals us.
Dying on the cross, he saves us.
Risen from the dead, he gives new life.
Living with you, he prays for us.
We praise you, eternal God,
through Christ your Word made flesh,
in the holy and life-giving Spirit,
now and forever.
Amen.[18]

Hymn: "Lord, We Have Come at Your Own Invitation" (*Presbyterian Hymnal*, no. 516)

God's Abundant Table

Just Eating

MAIN IDEA

From Deuteronomy to Acts, the Bible assumes that hungry people should be fed and that people should share what they have with those who do not have enough.

PREPARING TO LEAD

- Read chapter 3.
- Read this session and select questions and activities that you will use. What other questions, issues, or themes occur to you from your reflection?
- Each session includes a hymn. If you do not have a piano or keyboard and someone to play, consider asking someone to record the music so that the group can sing the hymn. Many prayers in worship will be taken from the Book of Common Worship, in particular from the "Great Thanksgiving" prayers. You may want to have a copy and review the sources.
- The readings and reflections for this week move from hospitality as something freely given or shared to social justice. How many schools have breakfast or lunch programs? How many children are eligible or take part? Do you live in a "food desert"? (Use a search engine like Google to find definitions and locations of food deserts.) Go to the Web site for Bread for the World and look at its statistics on hunger nationally and globally. Print out statistics on hunger either in your community or globally.

GATHERING

- Provide nametags and pens as people arrive.
- Enjoy simple refreshments; ask for a volunteer to bring refreshments next week. Ask everyone to bring canned/packaged goods next week to donate to a local food bank.
- If there are new people, remind everyone of the simple "ground

rules" and logistics (for example, time to begin and end session; location for meetings; welcoming all points of view; confidentiality; and so forth). Encourage participants to bring study book and Bibles.

OPENING WORSHIP

Prayer

Make us worthy, Lord, to serve our brothers and sisters throughout the world who live and die in poverty and hunger. Give them through our hands this day their daily bread, and by our understanding love, give peace and joy. Amen.

Lectio Divina (*reflective or prayerful reading*)

Read Matthew 14:13–21 aloud. Invite all to reflect for a few minutes in silence.

After reflection time, invite all to listen for a word or phrase as the passage is read again and reflect on that word or phrase in silence.

Read the passage a third time and ask all to offer a silent prayer after the reading.

Invite all who wish to share the word or phrase that spoke most deeply to them.

Prayer

Loving God, you open your hand and satisfy the desire of every living creature. Hear us as we pray today for all who are hungry (spoken prayers may be offered).

We thank you that you hear all the prayers of our hearts, spoken and silent. Hear us now as we pray together as Jesus taught us, saying, Our Father . . .

CONVERSATION

- Pass out handout on hunger (from Bread for the World Web site or another source). Discuss the issue of hunger and the needs of people for food in your community.

- What ministries does your congregation have that relate to hunger locally, nationally, or globally? Brainstorm possible hunger ministries.
- The story of the feeding of the multitude is told six times in the four Gospels. In the earliest Christian art, Jesus is portrayed not crucified on the cross but with baskets of bread and fish. This story was critically important to early followers of Jesus. Why do you think that might have been? One implication of the story is that where Jesus is, there is *enough and more*—enough to eat, enough room, enough love, enough life . . . and more left over. How would our lives be different if we believed that there would always be *enough* for us and everyone else?

CONCLUSION

Prayer

The Lord be with you.
And also with you.
Lift up your hearts.
We lift them to the Lord.
Let us give thanks to the Lord our God.
It is right to give our thanks and praise.
Grateful as we are for the world we know and the universe beyond our knowing, we particularly praise you, whom eternity cannot contain, for coming to earth and entering time in Jesus.
For his life, which informs our living,
for his compassion, which changes our hearts,
for his clear speaking, which contradicts our generalities,
for his disturbing presence, his innocent suffering, his fearless dying,
his rising to life and breathing forgiveness, we praise you and worship him.
Here too our gratitude rises for the promise of the Holy Spirit,
who even yet, even now, confronts us with your claims
and attracts us to your goodness.
Amen.[19]

Hymn: "You Satisfy the Hungry Heart" (*Presbyterian Hymnal*, no. 521)

SESSION 4

Food for the Spirit

MAIN IDEA

The Eucharist is one of the regular ways that our relationship with Christ is nourished, sustained, and deepened. Through the sacrament, we encounter Christ himself and are led to deeper lives of prayer, community, and service.

PREPARING TO LEAD

- Read chapter 4.
- Read this session and select questions and activities that you will use. What other questions, issues, or themes occur to you from your reflection?
- Each session includes a hymn. If you do not have a piano or keyboard and someone to play, consider asking someone to record the music so that the group can sing the hymn. Many prayers in worship will be taken from the *Book of Common Worship*, in particular from the "Great Thanksgiving" prayers. You may want to have a copy and review the sources.
- Read Sara Miles' book *Take This Bread: A Radical Conversion* (available in paperback).
- Sharing in the Lord's Supper is the means by which Christians should expect to meet and experience the Risen Christ. This week, participants are invited to reflect on various aspects of relationship with Jesus. Praying, meditating on Scripture, sharing the bread of communion, experiencing fellowship with others, and participating in service: all of these are means by which we can experience Christ. Helping group members to reflect on these means and explore those they may not have already experienced should be the goal of the time together.

GATHERING

- Provide nametags and pens as people arrive (especially if anyone is new).
- Enjoy simple refreshments and ask for a volunteer to bring refreshments next week.
- This is the midpoint of the study. Ask the group to reflect on their time together. Are there suggestions for doing things differently? Is the group willing to explore moving beyond study and conversation to a service project? Perhaps your church sponsors a food bank; the group could bring needed items. Perhaps there is a feeding program sponsored by churches in town; your group could volunteer to cook one week. Perhaps the children or youth group needs a meal or snacks; your group could provide those. Pick a project to do together, and then plan for a time before the study ends to reflect on your experience.

OPENING WORSHIP

Prayer

We thank you, Lord Jesus Christ, for your great love for us. Grant that we may know you more clearly, love you more dearly, and follow you more nearly, day by day. Amen.

Lectio Divina (*reflective or prayerful reading*)
Read John 21:15–19 aloud. Invite all to reflect for a few minutes in silence.

After reflection time, invite all to listen for a word or phrase as the passage is read again and reflect on that word or phrase in silence.

Read the passage a third time, asking all to offer a silent prayer after the reading.

Invite all who wish to share the word or phrase that spoke most deeply to them.

Prayer

Loving God, you feed us day by day with food for body, mind, and spirit. Hear us as we pray for the hungry, the lonely, the lost, and those in pain: (spoken prayers may be offered).

We thank you that you hear all the prayers of our hearts, spoken and silent. Hear us now as we pray together as Jesus taught us, saying, Our Father . . .

CONVERSATION

- Did any of the readings this week seem especially difficult or confusing? Share your questions, being prepared to live with uncertainty. The object is not so much to provide answers as to be open to questions.
- People describe their faith experience in different ways. Some speak of a deep sense of personal relationship with Jesus. Others talk more easily about God and God's presence in their lives. Still others feel a direct, ongoing connection to the Holy Spirit. However group members are comfortable expressing this, invite them to reflect on how the readings this week have caused them to experience God in new or deeper ways.
- In smaller groups of two or three, invite participants to share an experience of when the Lord's Supper was especially meaningful to them. What made it so? The circumstance? The setting? The service itself?
- One of the reflections this week reminds us that someone always brings the bread and fruit of the vine for a communion service. What else do we each bring with us? How do you prepare yourself for a celebration of the Lord's Supper? Ask group members to make a plan for how to prepare themselves for the next communion service they will participate in and share that plan next week.

CONCLUSION

Prayer

The Lord be with you.
And also with you.
Lift up your hearts.
We lift them to the Lord.
Let us give thanks to the Lord our God.
It is right to give our thanks and praise.

God's Abundant Table

Almighty God, you loved the world so much that in the fullness of
time you sent your Son to be our Savior.
Incarnate by the Holy Spirit, born of the Virgin Mary,
he lived as one of us, yet without sin.
To the poor he proclaimed the good news of salvation;
to prisoners, freedom;
to the sorrowful, joy.
To fulfill your purpose he gave himself up to death;
and, rising from the grave, destroyed death and made the whole
creation new.
And that we might live no longer for ourselves but for him who died
and rose for us,
God sent the Holy Spirit,
God's first gift for those who believe,
to complete God's work in the world,
and to bring to fulfillment the sanctification of all.
For this we praise and thank you, O God.
Amen.

Hymn: "Thee We Adore, O Hidden Savior, Thee" (*Presbyterian Hymnal*, no. 519)

SESSION 5

Giving Thanks

MAIN IDEA

The message of the gospel is God's grace—God's love abounding and everlasting available to all through Christ. The appropriate response for believers is gratitude. In the Lord's Supper, we receive God's grace, and we respond with thanks and praise.

PREPARING TO LEAD

- Read chapter 5.
- Read this session and select questions and activities that you will use. What other questions, issues, or themes occur to you from your reflection?
- Each session includes a hymn. If you do not have a piano or keyboard and someone to play, consider asking someone to record the music so that the group can sing the hymn. Many prayers in worship will be taken from the *Book of Common Worship,* in particular from the "Great Thanksgiving" prayers. You may want to have a copy and review the sources.
- This session invites participants to explore the Great Prayer of Thanksgiving (the prayer used at the celebration of the Eucharist) and through it, to reflect on various aspects of giving thanks. Cultivating an "attitude of gratitude" is a central practice for Christians. Gratitude should shape not only our everyday prayer life, but should inform the choices we make—for example, how we spend time and money and other resources. Gratitude is also the proper foundation for any discussion of Christian stewardship: we give not to support a budget or even to see good results; we give because we have received, because we are grateful.
- In preparation for the Lectio, get four sheets of newsprint and hang them around the room. After reading the psalm twice, invite participants to write on newsprint sheets and encourage them to walk around reading what others have written (allow ten minutes or so for this). Each sheet should be a sentence completion: "Today,

God's Abundant Table

I am grateful for . . ."; "The time I was most thankful in my life was when . . ."; "I find it hard sometimes to be grateful because . . ."; "I plan to show my gratitude more by . . ."

GATHERING

- If appropriate, provide nametags and pens as people arrive.
- Provide simple refreshments; ask for a volunteer to bring refreshments next week.
- Since this is the next to the last session, spend some time thinking about the closing session. If you have secured permission from your church's session, plan your celebration of the Lord's Supper. Divide up some responsibilities: select passage(s) of Scripture from the study to be read and assign readers; work with the pastor to select (or write) a Great Prayer of Thanksgiving; select and lead music; bake bread and bring wine or grape juice; prepare a table, thinking about appropriate colors, flowers, and symbols that reflect some of what you have talked about in this session.

OPENING WORSHIP

Prayer

O God, you have so greatly loved us, long sought us, and mercifully redeemed us. Give us grace that in everything we may yield ourselves, our wills, and our works, a continual thank-offering to you; through Jesus Christ our Lord. Amen.

Lectio Divina (*reflective or prayerful reading*)
Read Psalm 103 aloud. Invite all to reflect for a few minutes in silence.

After reflection time, invite all to listen for a word or phrase as the passage is read again and reflect on that word or phrase in silence.

After silent reflection, invite all to go to newsprint you have hung around the room and complete one or more of the sentences. Give ten minutes or so for people to write and reflect on what others have written.

Prayer

Blessed are you, strong and faithful God. All your works, the height and the depth, echo the silent music of your praise. Hear us as we thank you for all your goodness to us and to all creation: (spoken prayers may be offered).

We thank you that you hear all the prayers of our hearts, spoken and silent. Hear us now as we pray together as Jesus taught us, saying, Our Father . . .

CONVERSATION

- Reflect on the exercise of sentence completions and discuss some of the answers. Were some of the sentences difficult to complete? Why?
- Often people think of gratitude as an emotion (feeling grateful). But perhaps it is something different. How do you give thanks to God when you are in trouble or danger?
- The *Book of Common Worship* contains dozens of Great Thanksgivings that guide us on how to give thanks to God on different occasions: from ordinary Sundays to Christmas, Easter, and other special occasions; at weddings, baptism, funerals, and so forth. On page 156 there is an outline that suggests what should be included. Make a copy of this and hand it out to the group. Divide the participants into small groups of two or three persons. Assign each group one section of the prayer (if there needs to be more than three groups, more than one group can have the same section). Ask them to write in a few sentences that portion of the prayer. Have each small group read their work to the whole group.

CONCLUSION

Prayer

Holy God, we praise you.
Let the heavens be joyful,
and the earth be glad.
We bless you for creating the whole world,
for your promises to your people Israel,
and for Jesus Christ in whom your fullness dwells.
Born of Mary, he shares our life.
Eating with sinners, he welcomes us.

God's Abundant Table

Guiding his children, he leads us.
Visiting the sick, he heals us.
Dying on the cross, he saves us.
Risen from the dead, he gives new life.
Living with you, he prays for us.
With thanksgiving we take this bread and this cup
and proclaim the death and resurrection of our Lord.
Receive our sacrifice of praise.
Pour out your Holy Spirit upon us
that this meal may be
a communion in the body and blood of our Lord.
Make us one with Christ
and with all who share this feast.
Unite us in faith,
encourage us with hope,
inspire us to love,
that we may serve as your faithful disciples
until we feast at your table in glory.
We praise you, eternal God,
through Christ your Word made flesh,
in the holy and life-giving Spirit,
now and forever.
Amen.[20]

Hymn: "Now Thank We All Our God" (*Presbyterian Hymnal*, no. 555)

A Drama in Five Acts

MAIN IDEA

The Eucharist is enacted prayer. In the four actions performed by the minister or the one who presides at the table, the meaning of the Eucharist is on display. These actions in turn have resonance in our daily living and in our ordinary meals.

PREPARING TO LEAD

- Read chapter 6.
- Read this session and select questions and activities that you will use. What other questions, issues, or themes occur to you from your reflection?
- Each session includes a hymn. If you do not have a piano or keyboard and someone to play, consider asking someone to record the music so that the group can sing the hymn. Many prayers in worship will be taken from the *Book of Common Worship,* in particular from the "Great Thanksgiving" prayers. You may want to have a copy and review the sources.
- If you plan to celebrate the Eucharist to conclude your group study, you will need to secure the approval of your church's session and the leadership of your pastor.
- The reflections for this week are based on an insight from a noted liturgical scholar, Benedictine monk Gregory Dix, who helped shift theological attention away from the elements of bread and wine (and whether or not they "changed" in any way at the Eucharist) and onto the "four actions." In this way, he also called attention to how the Upper Room stories use the same words and phrases as we find in the story of the loaves and fishes, thus connecting the institution of the Lord's Supper to the whole of Jesus' ministry. As this study comes to an end, we examine the four actions as the heart of Eucharist and the implications of these actions for Christian life.

GATHERING

- If needed, provide nametags and pens as people arrive.
- Enjoy refreshments either as people gather or at the end of the session after the Eucharist (if you have made plans to do that).
- Whether you are celebrating Eucharist or not, set a table with plate and bread and a cup and beaker or pitcher. Place them on a table with a table covering appropriate to the season of the year (purple if it is Lent).

OPENING WORSHIP

Prayer

Almighty God, you provide the true bread from heaven, your Son, Jesus Christ our Lord. Grant that we who receive the Sacrament of his body and blood may abide in him and he in us, that we may be filled with the power of his endless life, now and forever. Amen.

Lectio Divina (*reflective or prayerful reading*)

Read Acts 2:42–47a aloud. Invite all to reflect for a few minutes in silence.

After reflection time, invite all to listen for a word or phrase as the passage is read again and reflect on that word or phrase in silence.

Read the passage a third time, asking all to offer a silent prayer after the reading.

Invite all who wish to share the word or phrase that spoke most deeply to them.

Prayer

God of all mercies, we give you humble thanks for all your goodness and loving-kindness to us and to all people. Hear our prayers: (spoken prayers may be offered).

We thank you that you hear all the prayers of our hearts, spoken and silent. Hear us now as we pray together as Jesus taught us, saying, Our Father. . .

CONVERSATION

- How was it helpful to reflect on the "four acts" of Eucharist? What new ideas did this spark for you? What did you think about the implications for how we think about leadership?
- The study suggests that the Eucharist is not an end in itself but rather continues as we take bread out (literally or symbolically) and share it with others. How might this be incorporated into worship in your congregation?
- If you did a service project together, this would be an appropriate time to reflect on that. How has this study helped you think about the connections among Eucharist, hunger, and the call to serve the poor?
- How can some of the ideas and practices in this study inform the way your congregation celebrates the Lord's Supper? Are there some recommendations you might like to bring to the pastor and session?

CONCLUSION

Scripture: John 6:35

Prayer

- If the session concludes with a Eucharist, select a Great Thanksgiving from the *Book of Common Worship;* for example, "C" on pp. 130–132. The minister then says the Words of Institution and the group serves one another by intinction.
- If the session does not conclude with a Eucharist, offer the Prayer of Thanksgiving No. 1 on pp. 158–159 in the *Book of Common Worship.*

Words of Institution

Sisters and brothers, the Holy Supper we celebrate is a feast of remembrance, of communion, and of hope. We come to remember that Jesus Christ was sent by God to live among us and to die for us. Through his death, resurrection, and ascension, Christ established a new and eternal covenant of grace, that we might be accepted by God, and never forsaken. We come to have communion with Christ, who has promised to be with us always. In the bread, he is the heavenly Bread, strengthening us to eternal life.

In the cup, he is the Vine in whom we must abide to bear fruit. We come in hope, for this bread and cup are a taste of the Supper we shall share with all God's people in the kingdom, when we are made like Christ in glory.[21]

Hymn: "For the Bread Which You Have Broken" (*Presbyterian Hymnal*, nos. 508, 509)

Prayer

Bless the Lord, O my soul;
and all that is within me, bless God's holy name!
Bless the Lord, O my soul, and forget not all God's benefits.
The Lord bless you and keep you.
The Lord be kind and gracious to you.
The Lord look upon you with favor and give you peace. Amen.

CELEBRATION

Enjoy food and refreshments together. Have joyful music to play. If the concluding service was not a Eucharist, pass the bread around for all to have a piece before you have other refreshments.

Notes

1. Daniel Homan, O.S.B., and Lonnie Collins Pratt, *Radical Hospitality: Benedict's Way of Love* (Brewster, MA: Paraclete Press, 2002), p. 21.
2. Sara Miles, *Take This Bread: A Radical Conversion* (New York: Ballantine Books, 2007), p. xi.
3. See Web site for Bread for the World, bread.org/hunger/us/facts.
4. Beverly Roberts Gaventa, *The Acts of the Apostles* (Nashville: Abingdon Press, 2003), pp. 111–116.
5. Martha Moore-Keish, *Do This In Remembrance of Me: A Ritual Approach to Reformed Eucharistic Theology* (Grand Rapids: Wm. B. Eerdmans Publishing Co., 2008), p. 144.
6. Kathleen Norris, *Amazing Grace: A Vocabulary of Faith* (New York: Riverhead Books, 1998), p. 271.
7. Sara Miles, *Take This Bread: A Radical Conversion* (New York: Ballantine Books, 2007), pp. 149–150.
8. Lawrence J. Johnson, *Worship in the Early Church: An Anthology of Sources, Vol. One* (Collegeville, MN: Liturgical Press, 2009), p. 37.
9. The *Qiddush for Sabbaths* in Johnson, p. 3.
10. *Book of Common Worship* (Louisville: Westminster/John Knox Press, 1993), p. 142.
11. *Book of Common Worship*, pp. 143–144.
12. *Book of Common Worship*, p. 145.
13. "I Greet Thee, Who My Sure Redeemer Art," in The *Presbyterian Hymnal* (Louisville: Westminster/John Knox Press, 1990), no. 457.
14. See Brian Gerrish, *Grace and Gratitude: The Eucharistic Theology of John Calvin* (Minneapolis, Fortress Press, 1993).
15. Gail Ramshaw, "Teach Us to Pray," in *Ordo: Bath, Word, Prayer, Table: A Liturgical Primer in honor of Gordon W. Lathrop,* ed. Dirk G. Lange and Dwight W. Vogel (Akron, Ohio: OSL Publications, 2005), p. 75.
16. For a list of some of the metaphors the church has used, see "The Confession of 1967," C-9.09 in *The Book of Confessions,* Presbyterian Church (U.S.A.).
17. *Presbyterian Hymnal,* no. 515. Words: Shirley Erena Murray © 1987 Hope Publishing Company, Carol Stream, IL 60188. All rights reserved. Used by permission.
18. *Book of Common Worship*, p. 152.
19. *The Worship Sourcebook* (Grand Rapids: CRC Publications, 2004), pp. 334–335. Reprinted by permission.
20. *Book of Common Worship*, p. 152.
21. Adapted from a liturgy of the Reformed Church in America by the Rev. Dr. Jeff Japinga (Director of Doctor of Ministry Programs and Continuing Education at McCormick Theological Seminary). Used by permission.